MC7-5

古樂風流

中國樂器

The Musical Arts of Ancient China

27.9.2001 – 8.1.2002

Jointly presented by

the Music Research Institute, Chinese Academy of Arts, the Department of Music
and the University Museum and Art Gallery of The University of Hong Kong

香港大學美術博物館、香港大學音樂系與中國藝術研究院音樂研究所　聯合主辦

香港大學美術博物館
University Museum and Art Gallery,
The University of Hong Kong

本展覽蒙北山堂基金贊助經費，特此致謝。
The University Museum & Art Gallery and the Department of Music of The University of Hong Kong are grateful to the Bei Shan Tang Foundation for its generous support.

古樂風流：中國樂器

編輯　　：蕭梅
　　　　　榮鴻曾
　　　　　黃燕芳
助理編輯：方敏兒
撰稿　　：蕭梅
　　　　　范俊英
　　　　　林晨
攝影　　：劉曉輝
　　　　　張麗華
圖錄設計：吳盈輝
出版　　：香港大學美術博物館
版次　　：二零零一年九月
印刷　　：Octo Plus
國際書號：962-8038-37-0

THE MUSICAL ARTS OF ANCIENT CHINA

EDITORS : XIAO Mei
　　　　　Bell YUNG
　　　　　Anita WONG
ASSISTANT EDITOR : Janet FONG
CHINESE TEXT : XIAO Mei
　　　　　　　 FAN Junying
　　　　　　　 LIN Chen
PHOTOGRAPHY : LIU Xiaohui
　　　　　　　　ZHANG Lihua
ENGLISH TRANSLATION : Bell YUNG
　　　　　　　　　　　 Tina PANG
DESIGN : Cynthia NG
PUBLISHER : University Museum and Art Gallery,
　　　　　　 The University of Hong Kong
EDITION : September 2001
PRINTING : Octo Plus
ISBN : 962-8038-37-0

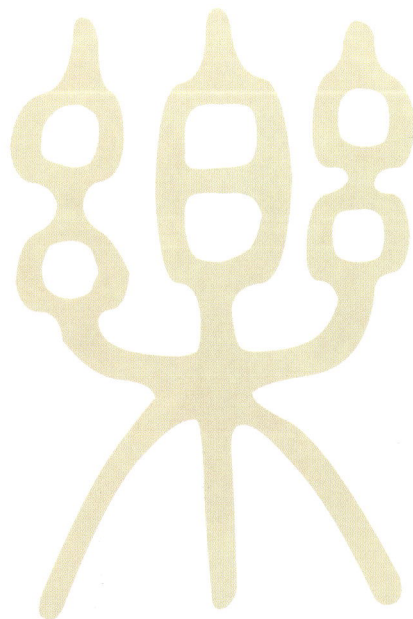

古樂風流

目錄 CONTENTS

古樂風流

前言

在古代的中國，"樂"是重要文化；國家的經濟、社會的風俗均可以從"樂"的風格反映出來。在穩定的社會，"樂"是平和的；在動盪的社會，"樂"是悲怨的。

"樂"其實是樂舞，將音樂、舞蹈、詩歌三者結合一起，成為日常生活中的重要環節。到了今天，樂舞的地位雖然不及從前，但這傳統文化是應該流傳下去的，千百年的歲月實在洗不掉所有喜樂悲歌。

從文獻，我們可以看到古時的詩歌。從繪畫，我們可以探索到昔日的舞姿。從樂器，我們可以聽到過去的樂聲。如果我們將文獻、繪畫、樂器三者結合研究，則古代的樂舞不難重演出來。若將文獻和樂器配合一起，則古代的樂曲可以再演繹出來。

在過去和現在，歡情、哀情、激情、柔情都是人之常情。萬般情意一一記錄在文學、繪畫、音樂等藝術作品上，給我們去細意感受和欣賞。

樂器如樂譜一樣，也是記錄音樂的工具。沒有樂器，音樂便失去聲音。

樂也如藝術品一樣，是記錄工藝技術的工具。銅鐘表現青銅藝術、陶塤反映陶塑功夫、石磬是雕刻的傑作、琴、箏、琵琶則綜合多種材料混化成出色的藝術品。沒有這些卓越工藝，樂器便訴不出動人聲音。

樂器亦是不可忽略的歷史材料。它們記錄漢族與少數民族的融和，例如南北朝時候，琵琶從絲路傳到中原。它們也記錄了中國與外地的交往，例如唐代琵琶東傳到日本，現藏於奈良的正倉院。它們甚至記錄了佛教的影響，質樸的木魚便敲出扣人心弦的梵音。

不同民族創作不同樂器，不同樂器奏出不同風格的音樂。這展覽便是選出中國樂器的精萃，把中華民族的演藝和工藝同時介紹出來，讓百樂共鳴，百藝共賞。

我們衷心感謝北山堂基金的慷慨贊助，中國藝術研究院音樂研究所和香港大學音樂系的鼎力合作，使我們的九十週年校慶更添色彩。

知音永在，餘音還留，歡迎您們到來這個中國人的音樂世界。

香港大學美術博物館總監

楊春棠

二零零一年八月九日於山之半館

FOREWORD

Music was an important component of ancient Chinese culture. The economy and customs of a community were mirrored in the style of music it produced: gentle in a peaceful society and sorrowful under unsettled conditions.

The Chinese term for "Music" actually refers to music for dance, a combination of music, dance and poetic verses which became an important aspect of daily life. Even though dance music is no longer as important to us today, this cultural tradition should rightfully be maintained, for time washes away neither the melodies of joy nor songs of sorrow.

Ancient poetry has been passed down in literary writings, dances have been recorded in paintings, and we are able to hear the sounds of the past through its musical instruments. If we were to study literary writings, paintings and musical instruments collectively, it is perhaps not too difficult to reproduce ancient tunes, and play again the dance music of the past.

Irrespective of the past or present, joy, sorrow, passion and affection remain common human emotions and are recorded in literature, painting and music for us to experience and appreciate. Like a musical score, an instrument is a recording tool; without musical instruments, there can be no music.

A musical instrument, like an art object, is a tool which documents the art it represents. A bronze *zhong* reflects the art of bronze; a pottery *xun* reflects the art of moulding clay, a stone *qing* is the art of carving; *qin*, *zheng* and *pipa* are art objects of materials combined. Without superb craftsmanship, these instruments would be unable to emit moving notes.

In addition, musical instruments are invaluable historical materials. They record the harmonious relations between the Han people and minority groups, and document cultural exchange between China and other foreign nations. *Pipa*, for example, were introduced into China during the Northern and Southern Dynasties via the Silk Road and later spread eastwards to Japan during the Tang Dynasty; an extant example is now in the Shōsōin in Nara. Buddhist influences may also be seen in the *muyu* which, simple and unadorned, produces Buddhist music that is touching to its listeners.

Different cultures make different musical instruments thus generating music of different styles. This exhibition features some of China's best musical instruments, to introduce to visitors the intrinsic art of the objects, as well as the art of Chinese performance.

We are truly grateful to the Bei Shan Tang Foundation for its generous support. Our thanks also go to the Music Research Institute of the Chinese Academy of Arts, and the University's Department of Music for its cooperation in making this event possible. All their efforts have added extra meaning to our celebration of the University's 90th anniversary.

Music lovers appear generation after generation. Moving music will always linger on. We extend our warmest invitation to each of you to come and share with us the musical world of China.

YEUNG Chun-tong
Director
University Museum and Art Gallery
The University of Hong Kong
9 August 2001

古樂風流

前言

在中國藝術的領域裡，音樂經常被人忽視，或被認為比不上歐洲的古典傳統，不能像詩詞、書畫、建築、陶瓷等讓中國人引以為豪。形成這種錯誤的觀點自有其複雜的歷史因素。一方面是近二百年來西方軍事，政治，及文化的入侵，使中國人對本土文化的自信心起了動搖。加上二十世紀初幾位受了西方音樂教育的中國高級知識份子、著書立論的抨擊中國音樂，左右了一般的輿論。

要糾正這種錯誤的觀念，最有效的莫過於利用教育，指出中國音樂光榮的歷史，及現存多彩多姿的豐富傳統。音樂是民族的集體聲音，是經過了世世代代樂人和聽眾們千錘百練所形成，包含了民族獨特的型態和風格。一旦民族的聲音埋沒了，民族也將失去了自己的個性。只有找回自己的聲音，才能真正的創造出光明的將來。

這次展覽會的宗旨就是教育，希望籍此能走出找回自己聲音的一小步。展覽會以樂器為重點，原因是樂器不單是音樂演奏的必需工具，它也包含了設計，工藝，和技術上的成就。中國古代把樂器分類為八音制：金、石、絲、竹、匏、土、革、木，更顯示出樂人對大自然物質聰明的採用和尊重。樂器除了給樂人發揮創作潛質外，也因它本身的特性而予以作曲家新的靈感。

這次展出的123件樂器及其他物件，都是北京的音樂研究所珍藏，包括好幾件從未在別處展出過的文物。展品大致可分為兩大類：其一是有歷史價值的古代器物，其二是音研所近幾十年在各地所搜羅的現代樂器，不少是來自邊陲少數民族，平時難得有機會見到。這次展覽兩類音樂文物能共濟一堂，更特出了中國音樂的深度和廣度。

這次大規模音樂文代展覽得以成功舉辦，端賴音樂研究所慷慨借出名下珍藏，以及香港大學美術博物館的專業陳列，更重要的還有北山堂基金的鼎力贊助。

香港大學音樂系群芳中國音樂講座教授

榮鴻曾

FOREWORD

Of all the traditional arts of China, music has generally been regarded as the weakest, pale in comparison with such illustrious sister-arts as poetry, painting, calligraphy, architecture, and ceramics. This view was promulgated mainly by Western-trained Chinese musicians and intellectuals of the early 20th century who knew little about the subject matter, and owing to political and social factors it still persists today. The only effective way to correct this biased and unfair assessment is to offer proper education and exposure, both formal and general, to the younger generation and the general public, as well as to our intellectual, political, social and business leaders. They need to be informed of the glory of China's musical heritage and the richness and diversity of the performing arts that are still in our midst. They need to be persuaded that the music of a people is its collective voice from the past, a voice that embodies its memories and feelings and speaks of its aspirations and hopes. To ignore or silence that voice will leave a people dumb, and if it is neglected too long the voice may disappear altogether and forever. Only by nurturing and promoting our collective voice will we be able to retain an identity and build a future.

This is the mission of the exhibition "Musical Arts of Ancient China", which, taking over three years to plan and implement, may well be the first ever of its kind in China. In selecting from the vast resources available, we have focused on musical instruments, for, short of the sound itself, an instrument reveals much not only about the music it can produce but also about the culture that has developed that music. In musical instruments we are able to recognize a synergy fusing design, craftsmanship, technology, and the sensitive adaptation of natural resources. Above all, musical instruments not only enable musicians to develop a distinctive voice, but also inspire them to explore new modes of expression by exploiting the instruments' unique capabilities and distinctive characteristics.

All of the one hundred and twenty-three instruments and other musical resources in the exhibition belong to the vast collection of the Music Research Institute of Beijing. Many of them have never been seen by the public before. The instruments can be divided into two large categories: those from the distant past, some dating to more than two millennia ago (with a few recent archeological discoveries among them), and those from the distant corners of the vast country, particularly rare instruments from the national minorities that are seldom seen elsewhere. As a whole, they offer a panoramic view of the depth of China's musical history and the breadth of its cultural richness and complexity.

This exhibition has been made possible by the generosity of the Music Research Institute in lending out its precious collection, and by the expertise of the University Museum and Art Gallery in mounting the display. The entire project was underwritten by the Bei Shan Tang Foundation, without whose generous support a project like this could never be realized.

Bell YUNG
Kwan Fong Chair in Chinese Music
Department of Music
The University of Hong Kong

古樂風流

前言

中國音樂是一條流淌了八千餘年的歷史長河。早在中華文明的曙光初現時，音樂就隨之發生了。

在至今猶存的音樂遺跡中，樂器、樂譜、樂書，共同記錄下中國音樂漫長的歷程和輝煌的過去。

通過二十世紀科學考古發掘出的各種古樂器，以它們無可懷疑的物質形態，透露出中國樂器的歷史信息：西安半坡遺址的"塤"，浙江余姚河姆渡遺址的"骨哨"，河南舞陽賈湖村的"骨笛"，將中國樂器產生的年代，由六千餘年前一直推到八千餘年；湖北隨縣的"曾侯乙編鐘"，更以其精美絕倫的工藝和完整豐富的鐘銘，體現了中國青銅樂器的雄渾、極致。總之，經過數千年的積累，中國樂器已成為世界各國樂器文化中最具民族特色的體系之一。

再者在"十三經"，"諸子百家"及"二十四史"等文史典籍中，保留了大量古代樂學、律學及歷代宮廷、寺廟、文人、民間音樂生活的寶貴文獻。如此詳實、不間斷的記錄，在全世界範圍內，應該是獨一無二的。

與文字記錄交相輝映的，還有中國的樂譜。為了錄載音樂這門特殊的藝術，古人先後創造了多種譜式，如宮商譜、律呂譜、古琴文字譜、古琴減字譜、管色譜、琵琶譜、工尺譜 (俗字譜)、燕樂半字譜、弦索譜、二四譜等約三十餘種。在中國音樂數千年的傳承中，樂譜起到了一種不可替代的歷史作用。

然而，樂器、樂書、樂譜，都是人的創造性勞動的結果。大而言之，它是中華民族獨創精神的結晶，是歷史上無數樂工、樂師、樂匠的反覆實踐的成果。小而言之，則是一代又一代傑出的演奏家、歌唱家、理論家們音樂智慧、才華的集中體現。

大致説來，要追溯中國音樂八千年的悠遠歷史，要揣摩中國音樂持續不斷的脈傳，樂器、樂書、樂譜、樂人，似乎缺一不可。

有鑒於此，我們選擇了以上四個方面，作為"中國傳統音樂文化展"這一主題的中心內容。

中國藝術研究院音樂研究所為中國大陸專事中國音樂文獻典籍、樂器、音響、圖片等資料收集、採錄、整理、研究的唯一學術機構，自1950年初創時期起，在楊蔭瀏等前輩的主持下，即致力於中國古代樂書、樂譜、樂器、圖片的收藏，保存和各民族、各地區存活音樂音響的採錄、整理。積五十年之時日，目前已收藏、保存了十五萬餘冊書譜、2100餘件古代或民間樂器、七千餘小時的採錄音響、四萬餘張唱片和五萬餘幅圖片。相對完整地為國家和全民族建立起一個"中國音樂資料中心"。本次音樂文化展，僅是本所收藏品的一小部分。但我們相信，它會以"管中窺豹，略見一斑"之效，讓親愛的觀眾步人中國音樂文化的偉大殿堂！

中國藝術研究院音樂研究所所長

喬建中

古樂風流

FOREWORD

The Music of China is an ever-flowing river of history that has lasted for more than eight thousand years. In the earliest days when the first Chinese appeared on this land, music was part of their lives.

The extant material of musical instruments, musicological writings, and musical notations record this long historical journey. They give testimony to China's glorious musical past.

Archaeological discoveries, particularly since the twentieth century, reveal a great variety of ancient musical instruments which provide indisputable evidence of the historical realities. Three notable recent discoveries are the *xun* mouth organ from the Banpo site of Xi'an in Shaanxi province, the bone whistles from the Hemudu site at Yuyao in Zhejiang province, and the bone flutes from Jiahu village of Wuyang county in Henan province. These and others pushed the earliest musical evidence from 6000 years to 8000 years in the distant past. The celebrated bell chimes of Marquis Yi of the State of Zeng from Sui county in Hubei province testify to the technological advances and exquisite workmanship of the Warring States period. After thousands of years of development, China has established a unique system of musical instruments with distinctive characteristics.

Among the voluminous historical writings from China's past, including such celebrated collections known today as the Thirteen Classics, the One Hundred Schools, and the Twenty-Four Dynastic Histories, were valuable records on musical life at court, in temples, literati circles, and among ordinary people. The depictions were concrete and detailed.

Complementing these words are direct representations of musical sounds and activities through specially created visual symbols. In order to record different kinds of music, our ancestors created no less than thirty kinds of musical notations, the most notable being the *gongshang pu, lülü pu, wenzi pu, jianzi pu, guanse pu, pipa pu, gongche pu* (or *suzi pu*), *yanyue banzi pu, xiansuo pu,* and *ersi pu*. These notational systems occupy a central position in our musical heritage.

The musical instruments, musicological writings, and musical notations are all products of the human mind and hand. They are the fruits of the wisdom and creative talents of innumerable musicians through the ages, the manifestations of tireless and unfailing spirits of experimentation, and the cumulative results of teaching and learning through countless generations of outstanding performers, singers, and theorists.

To comprehend the eight thousand years of China's musical heritage, one needs to note all four areas of source material: musical instruments, musicological writings, musical notations, and musicians. These form the guiding principle in curating this exhibition.

The Music Research Institute of the Chinese Academy of Arts is the only organization on the Chinese Mainland that is devoted to the collection of musical source materials that include musical instruments,

古樂風流

musicological writings and notations, sound recordings, and visual representations. From the day it was established in the early 1950s, the Institute, under the directorship of Yang Yinliu and others have made concerted efforts to seek out both historical and living materials from all the ethnic groups in the country for preservation and study. After almost fifty years, the Institute has accumulated one hundred and fifty thousand volumes of writings, 2,100 historical and living musical instruments, seven thousand hours of field recordings, forty thousand commercial disks, and fifty thousand photographs and other visual representations. It prides itself in being the national archive of Chinese music of all ethnic nationalities on this land. Although this exhibition presents only but a tiny fraction of our collection, it nevertheless opens a window through which to offer a glimpse of the glory of China's musical heritage.

QIAO Jianzhong

Director

Music Research Institute

Chinese Academy of Arts

古
樂
風
流

簡介

在歷史的長河中，中國樂器的品種可謂數不勝數。僅就半個世紀以來學者們搜集、整理，並仍流傳於民間的各類樂器及其變體，就不下千數餘種，更遑論那些沉眠於地下的歷史遺物了。"歷史悠久，種類繁多"這八個字，也許正是中國樂器相應於中國音樂文化寶庫的兩個特徵。

從文獻上看，中國遠古社會就有土鼓、陶鈴、鐘、磬、塤、簧、葦龠等擊、吹樂器以及琴、瑟等弦樂器的記載。到了周代，竟有七十多種樂器見於記載，並誕生了以金、石、土、革、絲、木、匏、竹這八種直接關係到樂器製作的發音材料為依據的"八音"樂器分類法。它不僅可以說是世界藝術史上對樂器進行的第一次系統分類，也隱藏了中國古人天象四時的自然哲學觀念、對發聲原理的認識、以及音色的審美追求等理想。

從考古實物而言，浙江余姚河母渡遺址中發現的骨哨迄今已有七千餘年。河南舞陽縣賈湖骨笛，距今也有八千餘年。從這些骨笛所鑽音孔以及鑽孔前刻劃等分所遺留的標記來看，這些上古樂器已經體現了製作者對音高的自覺要求及其與管長關係的認識。1978年，在湖北隨縣發掘的曾候乙戰國墓葬，出土了一套目前所見古代編製最為龐大的編鐘。其中的四十五件甬鐘，每一件的"正鼓"和"側鼓"部都能敲擊出兩個音，並鐫刻著它們的音階名稱。全套編鐘總音域跨五個八度，基調與現代的C大調相同。另外該墓葬還包括一套三十二件的編磬，一具面徑約九十厘米的"建鼓"，以及十弦琴，五弦琴、二十五弦瑟、簧、笙、排簫、不同形制的鼓等樂器。以這些樂器在墓葬中的不同分佈，如鐘、磬、建鼓居中室，竹木絲弦置東室來看，其堂上"鐘鼓之樂"與房中"琴瑟之樂"的不同配置，昭示了其時器樂藝術的成熟，並為中國音樂歷史上"禮樂制度"的見証。

"鐘鼓皇皇，磬管鏘鏘"、"戛擊鳴球"、"坎其擊擊"、"鼓瑟鼓琴"、"賁鼓維鏞"、"鼓瑟吹笙"、"如塤如篪"…描寫了先秦樂器及其樂器文化的燦爛。自漢以降，以"琵琶"為總稱的便攜式抱握彈弦樂器的發展，以及在中外文化交流中湧現出的橫吹之笛、笳、角、篳篥等吹奏樂器，銅鼓、羯鼓、腰鼓、毛員鼓、雞婁鼓、答蠟鼓等十數種鼓類打擊樂器，鑼，用定音鐵板製作的編組樂器方響，唐代出現的拉弦樂器等等，都隨著祀樂舞→ 歌舞伎樂→ 宋元俗樂→ 明清戲曲的歷史線索不斷豐富，並創造著中國樂器的發展。而廣泛分佈於中國邊疆的各少數民族，其擁有樂器的數量和品種更是多姿多彩。如果說樂器是文化的一個窗口，那麼，藉著鑒賞中國樂器，我們可以從中飽覽中國音樂、中國工藝、中國思想的斑斕景觀。

中國藝術研究院音樂研究所的音樂陳列室建立於1954年，目前藏有各歷史時期、各民族樂器兩千餘件。其中有來自梅蘭芳、程硯秋等文化名人的捐贈；有盛加倫、冼星海、鄭穎蓀等音樂家的遺物；還有本所幾代音樂學者跋山涉水，從邊疆民族採集的樂器品種；以及搶救於"大練鋼鐵"時代高爐前的打擊樂器；此外，本所還擁有八十餘張從唐至今，不同形制的古琴，如此集中的藏量對中國琴學而言可謂一筆豐厚的財富…。它們不僅構成了展示中國音樂風貌的基礎，每一樂器的來源和收藏經歷，亦可作為中國近現代乃至當代音樂史的生動史料。在此，我們按照氣鳴、膜鳴、體鳴、弦鳴的樂器分類，遴選其中的一百二十三件樂器參展，以饗那些熱愛中國音樂的人們。

中國藝術研究院音樂研究所陳列部主任

蕭梅

INTRODUCTION

It may be said that during the long course of history, Chinese musical instruments come in countless forms. It is barely fifty years since scholars have begun to collect and categorize China's extant musical instruments numbering over a thousand different types, not to mention those valuable objects that remained buried in the ground. Indeed, the two distinctive features of Chinese musical instruments are their long history and great variety.

From documentary records it can be seen that early Chinese society used various kinds of percussion and wind instruments such as earthen drums, pottery rattles, metal bells, chime stones, clay ocarinas, bamboo flutes, reed flutes as well as stringed instruments such as the *qin* and *se* zithers. By the Zhou dynasty, over seventy different types of instruments are recorded, and the "eight tones" or *ba yin* system of classification emerged using material, whether it be metal, stone, earth, skin, silk, wood, gourd, or bamboo as the principle of division. This is not only the earliest system of instrument classification in the world, it also reveals aspects of ancient Chinese thought. For example, philosophy, how people relate to their environment, their understanding of how sound is created, and the aesthetics of tone among others.

Archaeological sources include a bone whistle excavated from the site of Hemudu in Hangzhou, Zhejiang province and a bone flute from the site of Jiahu in Wuyang county in Henan province, over seven and eight thousand years old respectively. The drilling method of the holes, and the spacing of the marks that remain visible on these bone instruments of early antiquity marking where the holes should be drilled, show that the craftsmen of the time were aware of the relation between pitch and the length of the hollow.

In 1978, in Suixian County in Hebei, the Warring States period tomb of the Marquis Yi of Zeng (Zeng Houyi) was discovered. Among its contents was the largest set of *bianzhong* bells found thus far. The side and frontal parts of each of the forty-five *yongzhong* emit two notes when struck, and are carved with the names of the scales. The range of this set of *bianzhong* spans five scales and its fundamental set of tones is equivalent to the modern diatonic scale in the key of C. This tomb also yielded a set of thirty-two *bianqing* chimes stones, a drum of 90 cms in diameter, and zithers of ten, five and twenty-five strings, bamboo flutes, *sheng* and *paixiao* panpipes, as well as drums and other types of instruments. The way in which these instruments were arranged in the tomb prove that there was a familiarity with the art of musical instruments and that there was a system of ritual associated with music. The bells, chime stones and large drum were positioned in the central chamber indicating that they were used for public functions, while the instruments made of bamboo, wood, or incorporating silk were placed in the eastern chamber indicating that they were used in more private areas.

From early literature, phrases such as "the brilliance of *zhong* bell and *gu* drum, the clanging of *qing* chimes and *guan* pipes", "the striking and hooting of the earth", "the striking sound of percussion", "the striking of *se* and *qin* zithers", "the great *gu* drum and great *yong* bell unite", "strike the *se* zither and blow the *sheng* mouth organ", "as a *xun* ocarina, as a *ci* bamboo flute", and others not only describe the instruments of pre-Qin times, but also the splendour of the musical culture of the time.

From the Han dynasty onwards, due to active interactions with foreign cultures, a large number and variety of new instruments appeared. These include the plucked stringed instruments that were held when played, and collectively known as *pipa*; various wind instruments such as the sideblown *di* flute, the *jia* and *jiao* horns, and the *pili* reeded oboe; and various kinds of drums and other percussion instruments, including the set of tuned rectangular iron plates called *fangxiang*. During the Tang dynasty bowed stringed instruments appeared. All these instruments prospered and spread to many parts of the country along with the development of music and dance for ritual and entertainment, the rise of popular musical culture in the Song and Yuan, and the development of operas during the Ming and Qing. Furthermore, the many minority cultures of China's border regions have their own musical cultures with many distinctive types of instruments. If we are to say that music is but one window through which to view culture, then through appreciating the musical instruments of China, we can also learn about Chinese music, craftsmanship, Chinese thought and perceptions.

The Music Research Institute of the Chinese Academy of Arts was established in 1954 and up to now has collected over two thousand items covering all historical periods and minority cultures. The collection includes items donated by famous personalities such as Mei Lanfong, Cheng Yanqiu as well as items belonging to musicians such as Cheng Jialun, Xian Xinghai, Zheng Yingsun. There are also the musical instruments that several generations of musicologists from the Institute have travelled to the furthest reaches of China's borders to collect. And percussion instruments saved from the destruction of Mao's *Da lian gang tie* (the construction of thousands of backyard steel furnaces in place of large steel mills). In addition, the Institute has over eighty *guqin* zithers of different forms dating from the Tang dynasty to the present day forming an invaluable resource for the study of zithers. These not only express the foundations of style of Chinese musical instruments, but their origins, provenance, and collection history also provide vivid historical materials for the study of China's modern and contemporary musical history. We have divided the instruments according to the method by which they emit sound. The categories are aerophones (where the source of vibration is a body of air), membranophones (where the source of vibration is a stretched membrane), idiophones (where the source of the vibration is solid – often the entire body of the instrument), and chordophones (where the source of vibration is a stretched string). The 123 instruments in the exhibition have all been carefully chosen for those who love Chinese music.

XIAO Mei

Head of the Exhibition Department
Music Research Institute
Chinese Academy of Arts

古樂風流

中國歷史年代表
CHINESE PERIODS AND DYNASTIES

新石器時代	Neolithic Period	*c.* 6500–1500 B.C.
商	Shang Dynasty	*c.* 1600–1050 B.C.
西周	Western Zhou	*c.* 1050–771 B.C.
東周	Eastern Zhou	770–256 B.C.
春秋	Spring and Autumn	770–476 B.C.
戰國	Warring States	475–221 B.C.
秦	Qin Dynasty	221–206 B.C.
漢	Han Dynasty	206 B.C.–A.D. 220
西漢	Western Han	206 B.C.–A.D. 8
新朝	Xin Dynasty	9–23
東漢	Eastern Han	25–220
三國	Three Kingdoms	220–280
晉	Jin Dynasty	265–420
西晉	Western Jin	265–316
東晉	Eastern Jin	317–420
南北朝	Northern & Southern Dynasties	420–589
北朝	Northern Dynasties	386–581
南朝	Southern Dynasties	420–589
隋	Sui Dynasty	581–618
唐	Tang Dynasty	618–907
五代	Five Dynasties	907–960
遼	Liao Dynasty	907–1125
宋	Song Dynasty	960–1279
北宋	Northern Song	960–1127
南宋	Southern Song	1127–1279
金	Jin Dynasty	1115–1234
元	Yuan Dynasty	1271–1368
明	Ming Dynasty	1368–1644
清	Qing Dynasty	1644–1911

古樂風流

圖錄 CATALOGUE

樂器目錄 LIST OF EXHIBITS

體鳴樂器 IDIOPHONES

1 清鐘 *Zhong* (Bell)
2 清鐘 *Zhong* (Bell)
3 倍無射鐘 *Zhong* (Bell), tuned to the pitch of *Bei Wuyi*
4 先秦扁鐘 Pre-Qin *Bianzhong* (Flat bell)
5 大晟鐘 *Dasheng Zhong* (Dasheng bell)
6 鑾鈴 *Luanling* (Luan bell)
7 漢銅鈴 Han *Tongling* (Bronze bell)
8 方響 *Fangxiang* (Suspended metal xylophone)
9 虎鈕錞于 *Chunyu* with a tiger knob
10 商磬 Shang *Qing* (Stone chime)
11 清磬 Qing *Qing* (Stone chime)
12 虎紋大磬 *Daqing* with tiger engraving
13 鈸 *Bo* (Cymbals)
14 京鈸 *Jingbo* (Small cymbals)
15 蛙飾銅鼓 *Tonggu* (Bronze drum) with frog decoration
16 十二生肖銅鼓 *Tonggu* (Bronze drum) with twelve animals of the zodiac as decoration
17 帶紋銅鼓 *Tonggu* (Bronze drum) with engraved patterns
18 鐃 *Nao* (Large cymbals)
19 蛙式三系鑼 *Sanxiluo* (Gong with frog decoration)
20 大抄鑼 *Dachaoluo* (Large gong)
21 大鑼 *Daluo* (Large gong)
22 欽仔 *Qinzi* (Small gong)
23 金剛鈴 *Jingang Ling* (Small thunderbolt bell)
24 馬鈴 *Maling* (Horse bells)
25 木魚 *Muyu* ("Wooden fish" woodblock)
26 木魚 *Muyu* ("Wooden fish" woodblock)
27 拍板 *Paiban* (Clappers)
28 南梆子 *Nanbangzi* (Woodblock)
29 墜梆 *Zuibang* (Foot-operated woodblock)
30 平頭竹口簧 *Pingtou zhukouhuang* (Bamboo jaw's harp)
31 平頭竹口簧 *Pingtou zhukouhuang* (Bamboo jaw's harp)
32 劍形竹口簧 *Jianxing zhukouhuang* (Bamboo jaw's harp in the shape of a sword)
33 環形金屬口簧 *Qianxing jinshu kouhuang* (Metal jaw's harp in ring shape)
34 環形金屬口簧 *Qianxing jinshu kouhuang* (Metal jaw's harp in ring shape)
35 劍形金屬口簧 *Jianxing jinshu kouhuang* (Metal jaw's harp in the shape of a sword)
36 葉形金屬口簧 *Yexing jinshu kouhuang* (Metal jaw's harp in the shape of a leaf)

膜鳴樂器 MEMBRANOPHONES

37 土鼓 *Tugu* (Earthern drum)
38 雷鼗 *Leitao* (Lei-style tao-drum)
39 扁鼓 *Biangu* (Flat drum)
40 達瑪如 *Matigu* ("Horse's hoof" drum)
41 板鼓 *Bangu* (Clapper drum)
42 大鼓 *Dagu* (Large drum)
43 小堂鼓 *Xiaotanggu* (Small drum)
44 小堂鼓 *Xiaotanggu* (Small drum)
45 太平鼓 *Taipinggu* ("Peace" drum)
46 八角鼓 *Bajiaogu* (Eight-cornered drum)
47 蜂鼓 *Fenggu* ("Bee" drum)
48 點鼓 *Huaigu* (Lap drum)
49 額 *Shougu* (Hand drum)
50 南音扁鼓 *Nanyin biangu* (Flat drum for *Nanyin*)
51 撥浪鼓 *Bolanggu* (Drum)
52 細腰陶鼓 *Xiyao taogu* (Narrow-waisted clay drum)
53 瑤族長鼓 *Yaozu changgu* ("Long"drum of the Yao people)
54 沙鼓 *Shagu* ("Sha" drum)
55 狼帳 *Langgu* ("Wolf" drum)
56 秧歌鼓 *Yanggegu* ("Rice-planting song" drum)
57 花盆鼓 *Huapengu* ("Flower pot" drum)

弦鳴樂器 CHORDOPHONES

58 銅琵琶 *Tong Pipa* (Copper pear-shaped plucked lute)
59 五弦琵琶 *Wuxian Pipa* (Five-stringed pear-shaped plucked lute)
60 清阮 Qing *Ruan* (Long-necked plucked lute)
61 火不思 *Huobusi* (Four-stringed plucked lute)

62 忽雷 *Hulei* (Plucked lute)

63 小箜篌 *Xiao Konghou* (Small harp)

64 箜篌 *Konghou* (Harp)

65 瑟 *Se* (Bridged plucked zither)

66 五弦琴 *Wuxianqin* (Five-stringed plucked zither)

67 唱詞琴 *Changci Qin* (Zither to accompany poetry)

68 揚琴 *Yangqin* (Dulcimer)

69 清琵琶 Qing *Pipa* (Qing-dynasty plucked lute)

70 八角琴 *Bajiao Qin* (Eight-cornered plucked lute)

71 秦琴 *Qin Qin* (Qin-dynasty plucked lute)

72 雙清 *Shuangqing* ("Shuangqing" plucked lute)

73 柳琴 *Liu Qin* ("Willow leave" plucked lute)

74 玎膽 *Dingdan* ("Dingdan" plucked lute)

75 冬不拉 *Dongbula* ("Dongbula" plucked lute)

76 彈不爾 *Tanbu'er* ("Tanbu'er" plucked lute)

77 都它爾 *Dutai'er* ("Dutai'er" plucked lute)

78 熱瓦甫 *Rewapu* ("Rewapu" plucked lute)

79 莆田小三弦 *Putian Xiaosanxian*
(Small sanxian of Putian)

80 奚琴 *Xi Qin* (Bowed lute)

81 銅筒四胡 *Tongtong Sihu* (Four-stringed bowed lute)

82 提琴 *Ti Qin* (Bowed lute)

83 馬頭琴 *Matou Qin* ("Horse's Head" bowed lute)

84 京二胡 *Jing Erhu* (Bowed lute for Peking opera)

85 箏尼 *Zhengni* (Bowed zither)

86 牙箏 *Yazheng* (Bowed zither)

87 軋琴 *Ya Qin* (Bowed zither)

88 十三弦箏 *Shisanxian Zheng*
(Thirteen-string plucked zither)

89 十六弦箏 *Shiliuxian Zheng*
(Sixteen-string plucked zither)

90 伽倻琴 *Jiaye Qin* ("Jiaye" zither, or Kayagum)

91 古琴 (霜鐘) *Guqin* "Shuangzhong"
(*Qin* with name of "Frosted Bell")

92 古琴 (鳴鳳) *Guqin* "Mingfeng"
(*Qin* with name of "Cry of Phoenix")

93 古琴 (紅輕雷) *Guqin* "Hong Qing Lei"
(*Qin* with name of "Red Soft Thunder")

94 古琴 (雪江濤) *Guqin* "Xue Jiang Tao"
(*Qin* with name of "Snow River Tide")

95 古琴 (萬壑松風) *Guqin* "Wanhe Songfeng"
(*Qin* with name of "Wind in the Pines in
Ten Thousand Gullies")

96 古琴 (冰磬) *Guqin* "Bing Qing"
(*Qin* with name of "Ice Chime")

氣鳴樂器 AEROPHONES

97 十二律隔八相生管 Pitch pipes

98 彩塤 *Caixun* (Painted ocarina)

99 三彩釉陶哨 *Sancai*-glazed *Taoxiao*
(Three-colour glazed clay whistle)

100 怪異人頭瓦口哨 *Wakouxiao*
(Whistle made of baked clay in the shape of an ogre)

101 鬼頭塤 *Guitou Xun*
(Ocarina in the shape of a devil's head)

102 鳳簫 *Fengxiao* (Phoenix flute)

103 排簫 *Paixiao* (Panpipe)

104 龍頭笛 *Longtou Di*
(Flute with dragon's head)

105 龍頭弓笛 *Longtou Gongdi* (Flute in the shape of a
bow with dragon's head)

106 洞巴 *Dongba* (Reed pipe)

107 大管 *Daguan* (Large pipe)

108 小管 *Xiaoguan* (Small pipe)

109 海螺 *Hailuo* (Conch shell)

110 海螺 *Hailuo* (Conch shell)

111 方笙 *Fangsheng* (Square mouth organ)

112 十七簧笙 *Shiqihuangsheng* (17-pipe mouth organ)

113 銅簫 *Tongxiao* (Copper endblown flute)

114 銅笛 *Tongdi* (Copper sideblown flute)

115 鐵笛 *Tiedi* (Iron sideblown flute)

116 姐妹簫 *Jiemei Xiao* ("Sister" endblown flute)

117 尺八 *Chiba* or *Dongxiao* (Endblown flute)

118 曲笛 *Qudi* ("Opera" sideblown flute)

119 玉屏簫 *Yupingxiao* (Yuping endblown flute)

120 鷹骨笛 *Yinggu Di* (Eagle-bone flute)

121 鷹骨笛 *Yinggu Di* (Eagle-bone flute)

122 木嗩吶 *Mu Suona* (Wooden shawm)

123 小嗩吶 *Xiao Suona* (Small shawm)

樂器分類法

　　樂器展出的編排牽涉到樂器的分類法。這次展覽採取奧地利學者霍恩波士特(Hornbostel)及德國學者薩克斯(Sachs) 在 1914 年設計的分類系統，為世界公認為最具科學性及最客觀性，被學術界普遍沿用至今。分類系統的出發點是考慮到樂器發聲是因為樂器本身震動，而樂器震動是因為樂器一部份開始震動所致。分類的原則是把首先震動的部份分為固體、膜、弦，及氣。所分四類解釋如下：

體鳴樂器：這是指整個樂器的本身就是震動體，由其本身的固性與彈性受到震動弄出聲音，不需要張緊的膜或弦發聲，例如鐘和磬。

膜鳴樂器：聲音是由繃緊的膜激發而得，例如鼓。

弦鳴樂器：一至數弦張緊在兩個固定點間，受外來激發而出聲，例如琵琶。

氣鳴樂器：空氣本身是震動出發點，受外來激發而出聲，例如簫和笛。

CATEGORIZATION SYSTEM OF MUSICAL INSTRUMENTS

　　This exhibition uses a system devised by the Austrian Erich Moritz von Hornbostel and the German Curt Sachs in 1914. Considered the most scientific and objective, it has since been widely used in academic circles. The system is based upon the nature of material that is the source of vibration in the musical instrument. Briefly, the broadest level of the system divides all instruments into four categories:

Idiophone: in which the source of vibration is solid, which is often the entire body of the instrument. It does not require any stretched membrane or string to activate sound, for example a chime.

Membranophone: in which the source of vibration is a stretched membrane, for example a drum.

Chordophone: in which the source of vibration is a stretched string, for example a lute.

Aerophone: in which the source of vibration is a body of air, often trapped inside a cavity, for example a flute.

體鳴樂器 IDIOPHONES

1

清鐘

類型：打擊樂器

民族：漢族

製作年代：乾隆二十六年 (1761) 製。仿周代甬鐘制。

收藏年代：20 世紀 50 年代上海文物倉庫調撥。

樂器說明：銅製鐘狀，合瓦形。通高 71 厘米，鼓間 30 厘米，銑長 38.3 厘米。

演奏方法：編列敲擊

功能：古代宮廷儀典及宴饗之用。

Zhong (Bell)

Made in the 26th year of Qing Emperor Qianlong (1761)

Found among the Han people

Replica of a Zhou-dynasty *yongzhong*

H: 71 cm

Used in court ritual and entertainment music

2

清鐘

類型：打擊樂器

民族：漢族

製作年代：乾隆二十六年 (1761) 製。仿周代甬鐘制。

收藏年代：20 世紀 50 年代上海文物倉庫調撥。

樂器說明：銅製鐘狀，合瓦形。通高 68 厘米，鼓間 29 厘米，銑長 38 厘米。

演奏方法：編列敲擊

功能：古代宮廷儀典及宴饗之用。

Zhong (Bell)

Made in the 26th year of Qing Emperor Qianlong (1761)

Found among the Han people

Replica of a Zhou dynasty *yongzhong*

H: 68 cm

Used in court ritual and entertainment music

3

倍無射鐘

類型：打擊樂器

民族：漢族

製作年代：大明萬曆年 (1573–1620)

收藏年代：20 世紀 50 年代上海文物倉庫調撥。

樂器說明：銅製鐘狀，圓筒形，下端稍粗，平口。正面鉦間銘文"倍無射"，
背面鉦間大明萬曆年製。通高 27.2 厘米，鼓間 16.2 厘米。

演奏方法：敲擊

功能：學府、文廟之禮器。

Zhong (Bell), tuned to the pitch of *Bei Wuyi*

Made during the reign of Ming Emperor Wanli (1573–1620)

Found among the Han people

H: 27.2 cm

Used in ritual music in Academy and Confucian temple

4

先秦扁鐘

類型：古代打擊樂器

民族：古代巴人

製作年代：戰國 (公元前 475–221)

樂器說明：銅製鐘狀。合瓦形。通高 20 厘米，鼓間 4.4 厘米，銑長 13 厘米。

演奏方法：敲擊

功能：古代宮廷儀典及宴饗之用。

Pre-Qin *Bianzhong* (Flat bell)

Made during the Warring States Period (BC 475–221)

Found among the ancient Ba people

H: 20 cm

Used in court ritual and entertainment music

5

大晟鐘

類型：打擊樂器

民族：漢族

製作年代：北宋徽宗年間 (1101–1125)

收藏年代：20 世紀 50 年代上海文物倉庫調撥。

樂器説明：銅製鐘狀。此鐘律名為"中呂中聲"。鈕殘失。該器亦有後刻驗記
文字，但其位置處於"大晟"面的右側鼓部，為縱讀的"□□府□
□□□"。此外，大晟面正鼓部內壁有橫讀篆刻"王□□"，似為
後世收藏者姓名。鼓間 15.1 厘米，銑長 21.7 厘米。

演奏方法：編列敲擊

功能：音律準器、雅樂樂器。

Dasheng Zhong (Dasheng bell)

Made during the reign of Huizhong reign of Northern Song dynasty
(1101–1125)

Found among the Han people

D: 15.1 cm

Used in court ritual music and as a standard of pitch measurement

6

鑾鈴

類型：打擊樂器

民族：漢族等

製作年代：漢代 (公元前 206 至公元 220)

樂器說明：銅製棒狀，上端橢圓形球體內，置一小球。形似兒童玩具花棱棒。
通高 16 厘米。

演奏方法：搖之發聲

功能：置於舟車之上。

Luanling (Luan bell)

Made during the Han dynasty (BC 206–AD 220)

Found among the Han and other people

H: 16 cm

Attached to carriages and boats

7

銅鈴

類型：打擊樂器

民族：古代契丹人

製作年代：遼代 (916–1125)

收藏年代：20 世紀 50 年代上海文物倉庫調撥。

樂器說明：銅製鐘狀。呈合瓦形，通體鑄幾何圖案。通高13.5厘米，鼓身12.4厘米。

功能：懸掛於舟車馬具之上。

Tongling (Bronze bell)

Made during the Liao dynasty (916–1125)

Found among the Qidans

H: 13.5 cm

Attached onto carriages and boats

8

方響

類型：打擊樂器

民族：漢族等

製作年代：本所於 20 世紀 50 年代仿製。

樂器說明：鐵製片狀。上下兩層各八塊組成。每塊長16.1厘米，寬4.2厘米。以其厚
薄不同定音高，十二律具備。鐵製擊錘。

演奏方法：手握鐵錘敲擊

功能：曾用於宮廷燕樂，明、清時用於宮廷雅樂。

***Fangxiang* (Suspended metal xylophone)**

Made in the mid-20th century

Found among the Han and the other people

Replica of a Ming-dynasty instrument

L: 16.1 cm, W: 4.2 cm

Used in court ritual and banquet music during the Ming and Qing dynasties

9

虎鈕錞于

類型：打擊樂器

民族：古代巴人

製作年代：東漢 (25–220)

樂器說明：銅製容器形。橢圓筒形，肩圍大而腰圍小。鈕為虎形，仰首翹尾，
張口露齒，造型栩栩如生。通高 74 厘米、肩寬 44 厘米。

演奏方法：懸於橫木之上，執棰擊奏。

功能：《周禮·地官·鼓人》："以金錞和鼓"。金錞即錞于。多用於軍樂。

Chunyu with a tiger knob

Made during the Eastern Han dynasty (25–220)

Found among the ancient Ba people

Suspended from a beam and struck

H: 74 cm, D of shoulder: 44 cm

Used in military music

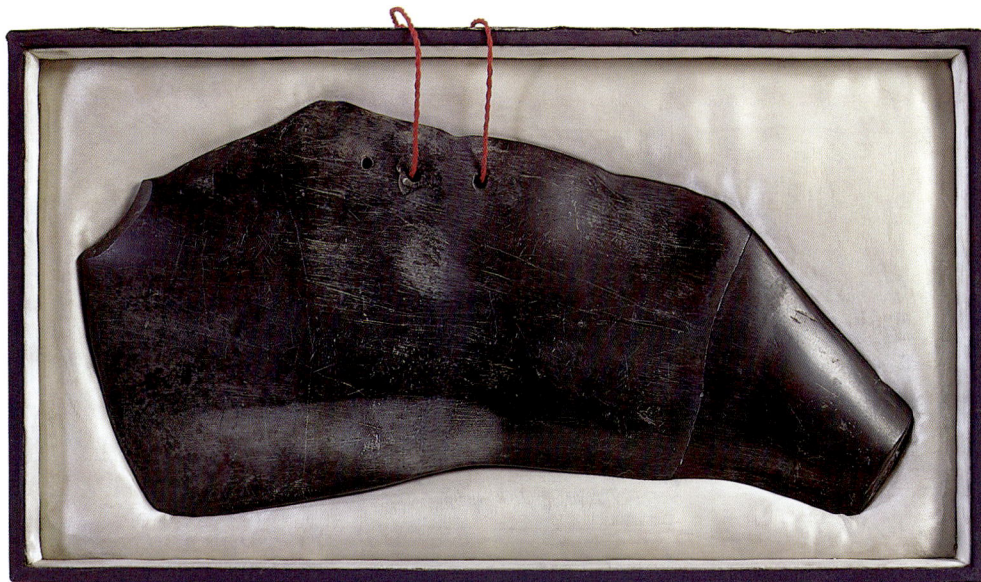

10

商磬

類型：古代石製打擊樂器

民族：漢族

製作年代：商代 (公元前 16 至前 11 世紀)

收藏年代：1963 年由浙江文史館金致淇捐贈。

樂器説明：石製片狀，不規則三角形。此磬石質黑色，表面磨光，是打製而成。
中殘斷，上鑽三孔，繫有紅繩。磬長 31.5 厘米，槌長 25.5 厘米。

演奏方法：手執木槌擊奏

功能："金石之樂"，主要用於古代祭祀、儀典、宴饗樂舞。

Shang *Qing* (Stone chime)

Made in the Shang dynasty (BC 16th–11th century)

Found among the Han people

Suspended from a beam and struck

L: 31.5 cm

Used in sacrificial rituals and banquet music

11

清磬

類型：打擊樂器

民族：漢族

製作年代：清代 (1644–1911)

收藏年代：原為鄭穎蓀舊藏，本所購於 20 世紀 50 年代。

樂器説明：石製片狀，呈不規則三角形。石材質黑，繪有山水人物圖案。
長 37 厘米，高 20.3 厘米。

演奏方法：手執木槌擊奏

功能："金石之樂"，主要用於古代祭祀、儀典、宴饗樂舞。

Qing *Qing* (Stone chime)

Made in the Qing dynasty (1644–1911)

Found among the Han people

Suspended from a beam and struck

L: 37 cm, H: 20.3 cm

Used in sacrificial rituals and banquet music

12

虎紋大磬

類型：打擊樂器

民族：漢族

樂器說明：石製片狀。此磬是河南安陽武官村晚商墓葬出土之虎紋石磬仿製品。
長 84 厘米，高 42 厘米。

演奏方法：手執木槌擊奏

功能："金石之樂"，主要用於古代祭祀、儀典、宴饗樂舞。

***Daqing* with tiger engraving (Large stone chime)**

Found among the Han people

Replica of a late Shang-dynasty instrument

Suspended from a beam and struck

L: 84 cm, H: 42 cm

Used in sacrificial rituals and banquet music

13

鈸　古稱銅鈸、銅盤，民間稱鑔

類型：打擊樂器

民族：漢族等

製作年代：大明宣德年 (1506–1521)

樂器說明：銅製乳凸形。凸部鑽孔，繫綢帶。乳凸上刻有"大明宣德年造"字樣
　　　　　及二龍戲珠圖案一周。其中一面乳部有殘。鈸面直徑34.2厘米，乳徑
　　　　　18 厘米。

演奏方法：雙手各持一面互擊，有輕擊、重擊、磨擊、撲擊等演奏手法。

功能：用於民間宗教、器樂、戲曲、說唱、歌舞樂隊及民俗活動中。

Bo (Cymbals)

Made in the Xuande period, Ming dynasty (1506–1521)

Found among the Han and other people

D: 34.2 cm

Used in religious rituals, and in instrumental ensembles, operas, storytelling,
as well as song and dance performances

14

京鈸

類型：打擊樂器。又稱水鑔。

民族：漢族等

收藏年代：20世紀50年代

樂器說明：銅製乳凸形。凸部鑽孔，繫綢帶。鈸面直徑19厘米，乳徑10厘米。

演奏方法：雙手各持一面互擊，有輕擊、重擊、磨擊、撲擊等演奏手法。

功能：用於民間宗教、器樂、戲曲、說唱、歌舞樂隊及民俗活動中。

Jingbo (Small cymbals)

Found among the Han and other people

D: 19 cm

Used in religious rituals, and in instrumental ensembles, operas, storytelling, as well as song and dance performances

15

蛙飾銅鼓

類型：打擊樂器

民族：彝、苗、瑤、侗、壯等民族。

製作年代：西漢 (公元前 206– 公元 22)

收藏年代：1958 年

樂器說明：銅製容器形。鼓腔中空無底。中心八芒，鼓面邊緣鑄六蛙飾，腰側各有對耳二個。面徑 103.3 厘米，高 51.5 厘米。

演奏方法：古代擊奏有平置地上和側旋兩種方式，現代則多用側旋擊奏。

功能：曾用以祭祀、宴享、傳信、賞賜或進貢。現主要用於伴奏銅鼓舞。

Tonggu (Bronze drum) with frog decoration

Made during the Western Han peiod (BC 206–22AD)

Found among the national minorities of the Southwest, including the Yi, Miao, Yao, Tong, and Zhuang

D: 103.3 cm, H: 51.5 cm

Used in ancient times for sacrificial rituals, entertainment, long-distance signalling, and as gift

Used in modern times mainly as accompaniment to song and dance performances

16

十二生肖銅鼓

類型：打擊樂器

民族：彝、苗、瑤、侗、壯等民族。

製作年代：明代 (1368–1644)

收藏年代：1958 年上海文物倉庫調撥

樂器說明：銅製容器形。上刻有十二生肖圖案。鼓腔中空無底。腰側各有對耳
　　　　　二個。面徑 49 厘米，高 29.2 厘米。

演奏方法：古代擊奏有平置地上和側旋兩種方式，現代則多用側旋擊奏。

功能：曾用以祭祀、宴享、傳信、賞賜或進貢。現主要用於伴奏銅鼓舞。

Tonggu (Bronze drum) with twelve animals of the zodiac as decoration

Made in the Ming dynasty (1368–1644)

Found among the national minorities of the Southwest, including the Yi, Miao, Yao, Tong, and Zhuang

D: 49 cm, H: 29.2 cm

Used in ancient times for sacrificial rituals, entertainment, long-distance signalling, and as gift

Used in modern times mainly as accompaniment to song and dance performances

17

帶紋銅鼓

類型：打擊樂器

民族：彝、苗、瑤、侗、壯等民族。

製作年代：宋代 (960-1279)

收藏年代：梅蘭芳舊藏，1953 年捐贈本所。

樂器說明：銅製容器形。鼓腔中空無底。腰側各有對耳二個。鼓面、鼓身飾卷
雲紋、回紋、連錢紋、乳釘紋等，足部飾三角垂葉紋。面徑 43 厘
米，高 25.8 厘米。

演奏方法：古代擊奏有平置地上和側旋兩種方式，現代則多用側旋擊奏。

功能：曾用以祭祀、宴享、傳信、賞賜或進貢。現主要用於伴奏銅鼓舞。

Tonggu (Bronze drum) with engraved patterns

Made in the Song dynasty (960–1279)

A gift from Mei Lanfang

Found among the national minorities of the Southwest, including the Yi,
Miao, Yao, Tong, and Zhuang

D: 43 cm, H: 25.8 cm

Used in ancient times for sacrificial rituals, entertainment, long-distance
signalling, and as gift

Used in modern times mainly as accompaniment to song and dance
performances

18

鐃

類型：打擊樂器

民族：漢族

收藏年代：傳世品。原為京劇大師程硯秋舊藏，1953 年捐贈本所。

樂器說明：呈圓形弧面，中央高於周邊。面徑為 43 厘米。

演奏方法：手執敲擊或安放在座架上演奏。

功能：用於民間宗教、器樂、戲曲、說唱、歌舞樂隊及民俗活動中。

Nao (Large cymbals)

Found among the Han people

A gift from Cheng Yanqiu

Held in hands or on a frame

D: 43 cm

Used in religious rituals, and in instrumental ensembles, operas, storytelling, as well as song and dance performances

19

蛙式三系鑼

類型：打擊樂器

民族：黎族

製作年代：明代 (1368–1644)

收藏年代：20 世紀 50 年代上海文物倉庫調撥。

樂器說明：銅製盤體。鑼上鑄有三個銅蛙形等距離繫繩孔。面徑 29 厘米，
臍 13 厘米，邊高 3 厘米。

演奏方法：繫繩懸掛，手執木槌敲擊。

功能：用於喪禮

Sanxiluo (Gong with frog decoration)

Made in the Ming dynasty (1368–1644)

Of the Li national minority

Suspended by three threads and struck with wooden stick

D: 29 cm

Used in funerary rituals

20

大抄鑼　又名篩鑼、黑鑼

類型：打擊樂器

民族：漢族

收藏年代：1959 年

樂器說明：銅製盤體。鑼邊、鑼心不刮光，呈黑色。面徑75厘米，邊高3厘米。

演奏方法：懸於木架，手執木槌敲擊。

功能：用於民間器樂合奏及游行慶典鑼鼓樂隊中。

Dachaoluo (Large gong)

Found among the Han people

Suspended and struck with wooden stick

D: 75 cm

Used in instrumental ensemble and in festive processional music

21

大鑼

類型：打擊樂器

民族：漢族

製作年代：清代 (1644–1911)

收藏年代：原為梅蘭芳舊藏，1953 年捐贈本所。

樂器說明：銅製盤體，又名低音冬字鑼。鑼面直徑 49 厘米，鑼邊高 11 厘米。

演奏方法：懸掛於木製鑼架上演奏。

功能：用於民間吹打樂及戲曲伴奏。

Daluo (Large gong)

Made in Qing dynasty (1644–1911)

Found among the Han people

A gift from Mei Lanfang

Suspended and struck with wooden stick

D: 49 cm

Used in wind and percussion ensembles and in opera

22

欽仔

類型：銅製打擊樂器

民族：漢族

收藏年代：20 世紀 60 年代

樂器說明：銅製乳凸形。是乳鑼之一種。流行於廣東潮州、汕頭地區。
鑼面直徑 25 厘米，鑼邊寬 3 厘米。

演奏方法：用木槌敲擊中央部分振動發音。

功能：用於潮州大鑼鼓和潮劇伴奏。

Qinzi (Small gong)

Found among the Han people

Knobbed gong from the South-eastern coastal area

D: 25 cm

Used in Chaozhou opera and Chaozhou percussion ensemble

23

金剛鈴

類型：打擊樂器

民族：藏、蒙古、納西、漢等民族。

製作年代：清乾隆年間 (1736–1795)

收藏年代：1958 年

樂器說明：銅製鐘狀。呈倒懸杯形，下口圓，鈴身內懸有銅製鈴
舌。鈴柄裝飾繁縟，鑄有佛像，刻有 "乾隆年造" 四
字。通高 22 厘米。

演奏方法：手執鈴柄搖奏

功能：藏傳佛教法器，亦見用於納西族洞經音樂等。

Jingang Ling (**Small thunderbolt bell**)

Made in the Qianlong period (1736–1795) of Qing dynasty

Found among the Tibetan, Mongolian, Naxi, and Han people

Played by shaking

H: 22 cm

Used in Tibetan Buddhist rituals and in Naxi Dongjing rituals

古樂風流

24

馬鈴

類型：打擊樂器

民族：藏、納西、土家等民族。

收藏年代：傳世品。原為京劇大師梅蘭芳收藏，1953 年捐贈。

樂器說明：銅製球狀。由三個高 10.5 厘米，圓徑 9.2 厘米內置小球的銅鈴組成。

功能：為少數民族民間宗教祭祀、樂舞擊節之用。

Maling **(Horse bells)**

A gift from Mei Lanfang

Found among the Tibetan, Naxi and Tujia people

Three metallic hollow spheres each with a metal pellet inside

H: 10.5 cm, C: 9.2 cm

Used in religious rituals as well as song and dance performances

25

木魚

類型：打擊樂器

民族：漢族

收藏年代：1959 年

樂器説明：木製槽狀。呈團魚形，腹部中空，頭部正中開口，尾部盤繞，其狀昂
首縮尾，背部呈斜坡形，兩側三角形，底部橢圓，正面圓徑 48.5 厘
米。木製棰，長 50 厘米。

演奏方法：手執木棰擊奏

功能：用於佛教法事、念誦。

Muyu ("Wooden fish" woodblock)

Found among the Han people

C: 48.5 cm

Used in Buddhist rituals and chanting

26

木魚

類型：打擊樂器

民族：漢族

收藏年代：傳世品。梅蘭芳舊藏，1953年捐贈。

樂器說明：木製槽狀。正面圓徑25厘米。木製槌，長22厘米。

演奏方法：手執木槌擊奏

功能：用於佛教法事、念誦。

***Muyu* ("Wooden fish" woodblock)**

A gift from Mei Lanfang

Found among the Han people

C: 25 cm

Used in Buddhist rituals and chanting

27

拍板　又稱檀板、綽板，簡稱板

類型：打擊樂器

民族：漢族

收藏年代：傳世唐製古板。原為京劇大師梅蘭芳收藏，1953年捐贈本所。

樂器說明：木製板狀。六塊。板呈梯形，上寬6.9厘米，下寬8厘米，厚1.4厘米。
　　　　　前後用布帶連結。

演奏方法：擊奏時，左手持外板，使其下端凸起部分撞擊前三塊木板背面發聲。

功能：用於戲曲、說唱伴奏及器樂合奏。

Paiban (Clappers)

Made in the Tang dynasty (618–907)

A gift from Mei Lanfang

Found among the Han people

W: 6.9–8 cm, T: 1.4 cm

Used in opera, storytelling, and instrumental ensemble

28

南梆子 又名卜魚、廣東板

類型：打擊樂器

民族：漢族

收藏年代：1960年代

樂器說明：木製槽體。中間雙面開長條形窄縫音孔，內腔漸大。長21厘米，
寬7.8厘米，厚6.4厘米。

演奏方法：左手持梆，右手執一竹籤或木槌敲擊。

功能：原用於粵劇伴奏和廣東音樂演奏，後也用於京劇樂隊和器樂合奏，還可
作馬蹄聲效果。

Nanbangzi (Woodblock)

Found among the Han people

L: 21 cm, W: 7.8 cm, T: 6.4 cm

Used mainly among the Cantonese community to accompany Cantonese
opera and in instrumental ensembles

29

墜梆 又稱腳踏梆子

類型：打擊樂器

民族：漢族

收藏年代：1958 年

樂器説明：木製球狀。形如鴨蛋，圓徑 9 厘米，中空。全長 80.5 厘米。腰部有一木榫，垂直固定在一個立棍上。下方另置一榫槽，中心橫穿一軸，分別連接擊梆木槌與拉繩。

演奏方法：繩繫於奏者右腳上，通過腳踩動，控製木槌擊梆發音。演奏時常將立棍綁在桌腿上，由操墜胡者兼奏。

功能：用於豫劇及河南墜子書伴奏。

Zuibang (Foot-operated woodblock)

Found among the Han people

L: 80.5 cm

The beater of the woodblock is tied to the right foot of the performer, who would be playing the *zui*-bowed lute at the same time

Used mainly to accompany Henan opera and Henan storytelling

30

平頭竹口簧　又稱口琴、口弦、響篾、彈篾、吹篾等

類型：撥奏樂器

民族：彝、藏、羌、栗僳、怒等民族。

收藏年代：20世紀50年代

樂器説明：竹製框架單個自體簧。平頭，通長14厘米，簧長10.5厘米。

演奏方法：將簧舌部分執於兩唇間，以右手拇指、食指彈擊頭部，引起簧舌振動
　　　　　發音。

功能：自娛、社交與愛情生活。

Pingtou zhukouhuang (Bamboo jaw's harp)

Found among the Tibetans, Yi, Jiang, Sulu, Nu, and other national minorities

L: 14 cm

Used for courtship and other social occasions

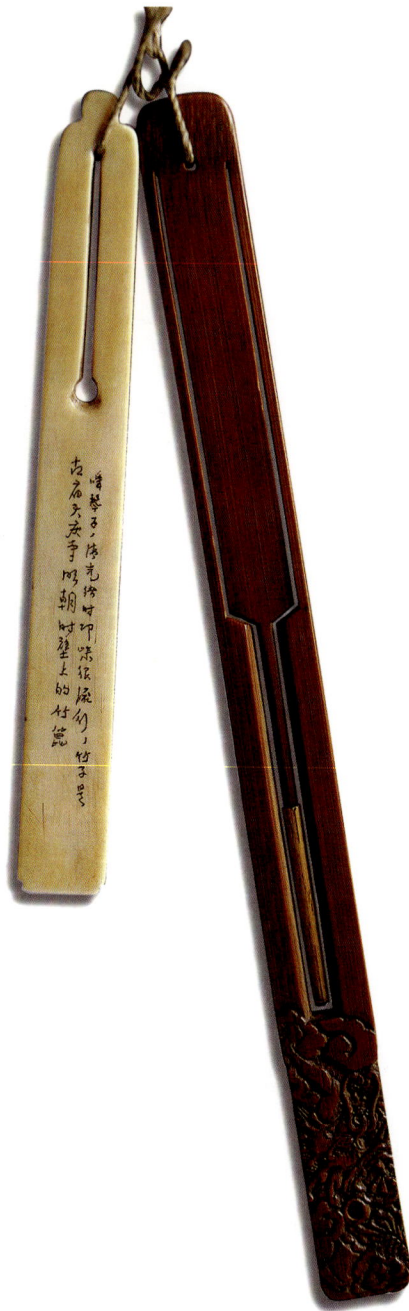

31

平頭竹口簧　又稱口琴、口弦、響篾、彈篾、吹篾等

類型：撥奏樂器

民族：彝、藏、羌、栗僳、怒等民族。

收藏年代：1951年川西人民文化館捐贈。

樂器說明：竹製框架單個自體簧體。平頭，通長14.5厘米。

演奏方法：將簧舌部分執於兩唇間，以右手拇指、食指彈擊
　　　　　頭部，引起簧舌振動發音。

功能：自娛、社交與愛情生活。

Pingtou zhukouhuang (**Bamboo jaw's harp**)

Found among the Tibetans, Yi, Jiang, Sulu, Nu, and
other national minorities

L: 14.5 cm

Used for courtship and other social occasions

32

劍形竹口簧　又稱拉篾、拉線竹簧

類型：扯奏樂器

民族：彝、拉祜、栗僳、布朗、景頗等民族。

收藏年代：1965 年宁夏代表團贈。

樂器説明：竹製框架單個自體簧。劍頭，通長 13.3 厘米。

演奏方法：將頭部絲線纏於右手，食指、中指拉動引線，使簧舌振動發音。

功能：自娛、社交與愛情生活。

Jianxing zhukouhuang (Bamboo jaw's harp in the shape of a sword)

Found among the Yi, Lagu, Sulu, Bulang, Jingpo and other national minorities

The right hand index and middle fingers pull a string that is attached to the reed to activate the instrument

L: 13.3 cm

Used for courtship and other social occasions

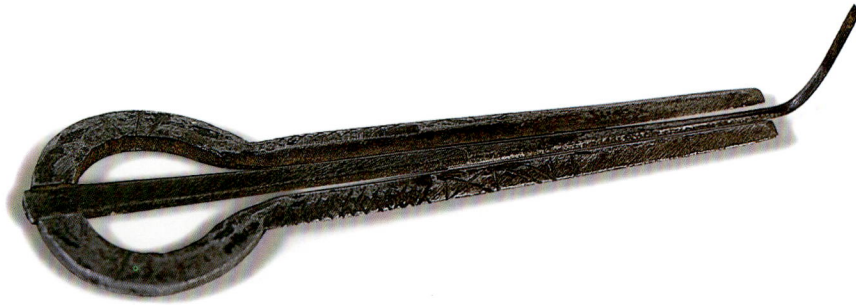

33

環形金屬口簧　又稱口胡、木庫連等

類型：撥奏樂器

民族：東北各民族。

收藏年代：1963 年內蒙古音協贈送。

樂器說明：鐵製框架單個异體簧。鉗形，長 10.5 厘米。

演奏方法：左手執簧架，將固定簧舌的一端置於齒間，簧舌露於唇外，右手食指撥動簧尖發音。

功能：自娛、社交與愛情生活。多用於女性。

Huanxing jinshu kouhuang (Metal jaw's harp in ring shape)

Found among the North-eastern national minorities

L: 10.5 cm

Used for courtship and other social occasions

Played mainly by women

34

環形金屬口簧　又稱口胡、木庫連琴等

類型：撥奏樂器

民族：東北各民族。

收藏年代：1963 年內蒙古音協贈送。

樂器說明：鐵製框架單個異體簧。鉗形，帶花紋小木盒。長 6.6 厘米。

演奏方法：左手執簧架，將固定簧舌的一端置於齒間，簧舌露於唇外，右手食指撥動簧尖，口腔同時哈氣哼鳴共振發音。

功能：自娛、社交與愛情生活。多用於女性。

Huanxing jinshu kouhuang (Metal jaw's harp in ring shape)

Found among the North-eastern national minorities

L: 6.6 cm

Used for courtship and other social occasions

Played mainly by women

35

劍形金屬口簧 又稱銅口簧，苗語為 "卡誰"、"會將"、"加" 等

類型：撥奏樂器

民族：苗族

收藏年代：傳世品。 1999 年購於貴州黔西縣化屋基村。

樂器說明：銅製框架單個自體簧。劍形，帶花紋圓竹筒盒。全長4.75厘米，舌長2.55厘米。

演奏方法：左手執琴尾，橫置於口，簧舌置上下唇間，右手拇指撥簧，口腔同時哈氣哼鳴共
振發音。

功能：自娛、社交與愛情生活。多用於女性。

Jianxing jinshu kouhuang (Metal jaw's harp in the shape of a sword)

Found among the Miao national minority

Origin unknown, purchased in Guizhou province

L: 4.75 cm

Used for courtship and other social occasions

Played mainly by women

36

葉形金屬口簧　古稱鐵葉簧

類型：撥奏樂器

民族：彝、拉祜、哈尼、基諾等民族。

收藏年代：20世紀50年代

樂器說明：銅製框架多個自體簧。葉形，兩邊簧框內卷，構成葉柄，簧舌成三角形。長8.2厘米，舌長5.4厘米。

演奏方法：多片簧用繩穿在一起撥奏。

功能：自娛、社交與愛情生活。多用於女性。

Yexing jinshu kouhuang (Metal jaw's harp in the shape of a leaf)

Found among the Yi, Lagu, Hani, Jinuo and other national minorities

L: 8.2 cm

Used for courtship and other social occasions

Played mainly by women

膜鳴樂器 MEMBRANOPHONES

37

土鼓

類型：打擊樂器

民族：古代西北民族

製作年代：新石器時代

收藏年代：原為青海師範大學梁今知教授收藏，1998 年捐贈本所。

樂器說明：陶製沙漏形。兩端粗，中腰細，一端呈罐狀，一端呈敞口喇叭狀，
大小口相通，口外側邊沿有對稱環耳。鼓腔全長 20 厘米，大端口徑
18 厘米，小端口徑 8.4 厘米。

Tugu (Earthern drum)

Used by ancient north-western tribes

Made during the Neolithic period

L: 20 cm, D: 8.4–18 cm

38

雷鼗

類型：打擊樂器

民族：漢族

收藏年代：本品仿雷鼗古制。原為京劇大師程硯秋舊藏，
　　　　　並 於 1953 年捐贈本所。

樂器說明：由面徑為 12 厘米，長 26 厘米，腰徑 17 厘米的
　　　　　四鼓八面組成，中由 194 厘米長的木杖串起，
　　　　　插入鼓架，頂端雕有鳥飾及蓮花。底架長 5 6
　　　　　厘米，寬 36 厘米，高 55 厘米。

演奏方法：雙手持鼓杖搖奏

功能：《正義》：《周禮·小師》注云："鼗，如鼓，而小
　　　持其柄搖之旁耳還自擊"。此謂鼗與擊奏鼓之別。
　　　又，《周禮·地官》："以雷鼓鼓神祀"。鄭康成
　　　注："雷鼓，八面鼓也；神祀，祀天神也。

Leitao (**Lei-style tao-drum**)

Replica of ancient sample

A gift from Cheng Yanqin

Found among the Han people

An eight-faced drum (hence Lei-style) resting on a
tall staff

Played by rotating the staff briskly

D: 12 cm

Used in sacrificial rituals

39

扁鼓

類型：打擊樂器

民族：古代楚人

收藏年代：仿戰國古制傳世品。 1959 年湖南省博物館轉撥本所。

樂器説明：雙面固定框狀。鼓腔椴木製，通施彩繪紋飾，並置有三環，兩面蒙牛
皮。面徑 52 厘米，鼓高 23 厘米，腰徑 58 厘米。

演奏方法：懸掛擊奏

功能：古代用於宮廷祭祀、儀典、宴饗。

Biangu (Flat drum) from the Chu kingdom in pre-Qin times

Replica of sample from the Warring States Period (BC 475–221)

Used by ancient Chu people

Suspended from a beam and struck

D: 52 cm

Used in court sacrificial rituals and banquet music

40

達瑪如　又稱馬蹄鼓、丹不楞兒 (蒙)

類型：打擊樂器

民族：藏族、蒙古族

收藏年代：1958 年

樂器說明：雙面固定沙漏形。鼓腔用硬木製作，兩面蒙人皮。對稱的兩側各繫一絨布細繩，其盡端
　　　　　有球形硬質小鼓墜。鼓腰拴繫彩緞、絲穗為飾。鼓體高 9.7 厘米，面徑 12.3 厘米。

演奏方法：右手執鼓，用拇指、食指執其細腰部位，中指、無名指、小指托住彩帶，搖晃手腕，小
　　　　　鼓墜敲擊鼓面而發聲。

功能：寺院誦經活動及民間熱巴鈴鼓舞。

Matigu ("Horse's hoof" drum)

Found in Tibet and Mongolia

Hour-glass shaped wooden frame with human skin for the two drum faces, with wooden
pellets tied to ribbons hung from the side

Played by holding the drum at the drum waist and twisting the drum back and forth to let
the pellets hit the drum faces

D: 12.3 cm, H: 9.7 cm

Used in Buddhist chanting and in social song and dance performances

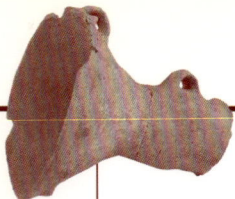

41

板鼓　又名班鼓、邊鼓、單皮、小鼓、崩子鼓、環鼓等

類型：打擊樂器

民族：漢族

收藏年代：20世紀50年代初

樂器說明：單面框架形。鼓身用五塊較厚木板拼合而成，扁狀。鼓皮張緊於鼓面並包到鼓身底端，用密排鼓釘繃緊，底部並箍以鐵圈。鼓腔呈八字形，鼓身直徑25厘米，邊高9.5厘米。

演奏方法：將鼓吊於木架上，用兩根藤或竹製鼓箭敲擊。有單打、雙打、悶打等手法。

功能：主要用於戲曲伴奏及民間器樂合奏。

Bangu (Clapper drum)

Found among the Han people

Suspended on a wooden frame and struck with two bamboo or rattan beaters

D: 25 cm, H: 9.5 cm

Used mainly in operas and instrumental ensembles

42

大鼓

類型：打擊樂器

民族：漢族

收藏年代：原為京劇大師程硯秋舊藏，1958 年捐贈本所。

樂器說明：固定雙面桶形。通體髹紅漆，有描金的鳳凰、牡丹圖案。腔體上有兩
排鐵釘。面徑 38 厘米，鼓腔高 71 厘米，腰徑 54 厘米，膜寬 6.5 厘米。

演奏方法：手執鼓槌擊奏，有單打、雙打、滾擊、悶擊等技巧。

功能：用於民間器樂合奏及歌舞、戲曲伴奏和喜慶節日群眾性的鑼鼓樂隊中。

Dagu (Large drum)

Found among the Han people

A gift from Cheng Yanqiu

Barrel-shaped drum is suspended on a wooden frame and struck with a pair of wooden beaters

D: 38 cm, H: 71 cm

Used in instrumental ensembles to accompany operas, song and dance performances, and in festival occasions

43

小堂鼓

類型：打擊樂器

民族：漢族

收藏年代：傳世品。原為京劇大師梅蘭芳收藏，1953 年捐贈本所。

樂器說明：固定雙面桶形。腔體置四銅環，兩排鐵釘。通體髹黑漆，繪描金雲紋
圖案。面徑 34 厘米，鼓腔高 35.5 厘米，腰徑 45 厘米，膜寬 3.7 厘米。

演奏方法：將鼓空懸於木製三角架上，用木製雙棰直接敲擊。通過敲擊鼓邊、
鼓心、鼓框以及力度的控制，變化音色。

功能：用於民間器樂合奏。舞蹈、戲曲伴奏和喜慶節日群眾性的鑼鼓隊中。

Xiaotanggu (Small drum)

Found among the Han people

A gift from Mei Lanfang

Barrel-shaped drum is suspended from a wooden frame and struck with a pair of wooden beaters

D: 34 cm, H: 35.5 cm

Used in instrumental ensembles to accompany operas, song and dance performances, and in festival occasions

44

小堂鼓 俗稱 "鬧喪鼓子"

類型：打擊樂器

民族：漢族

收藏年代：1958 年

樂器說明：固定雙面桶形。鼓身外表以燙金花紋圖案為飾。面徑10厘米、高40厘米。

演奏方法：一人於鼓環中繫帶掛於背上，另一人在其後執雙槌敲擊，多在行進中演奏。

功能：舊時在中國北方地區用於民間喪事活動。

Xiaotanggu (Small drum, also known as Funerary drum)

Found among the Han people

Barrel-shaped drum is hung on one person's back and beaten by a second person

D: 10 cm, H: 40 cm

Used in processional music for funerary rites

45

太平鼓 又名扇鼓、羊皮鼓、喜子鼓

類型：打擊樂器

民族：滿族、蒙古族、漢族

收藏年代：1958 年

樂器說明：單面框架。鼓面呈橢圓形，在鐵圈製鼓框上蒙以羊皮。皮面光素，鐵圈四
周繫有數個絨球為飾，鼓柄下端綴有數枚小鐵環。鼓槌稱鼓鞭，竹製。鼓
高 54.4 厘米，鼓徑 30.5 厘米。

演奏方法：左手執鼓柄，右手執鼓鞭敲擊鼓面，並同時振動鐵環作響。

功能：多用於舞蹈伴奏，邊敲邊舞。常在農曆正月新春或元宵佳節等喜慶活動中表演。

Taipinggu (**"Peace" drum**)

Found among the Manchurians, Mongolians, and the Han people

Single-faced frame drum with sheep skin and a short handle hung with metal rings

Played by holding the handle with left hand and beating the drum surface with the right hand with a bamboo drum beater

D: 30.5 cm, H: 54.4 cm

Used to accompany song and dance performances during festivities

46

八角鼓

類型：打擊樂器

民族：漢、滿、白等民族。

收藏年代：1958 年

樂器說明：固定單面框架。鼓身較小，框為紅木製八角形。蒙以蟒皮，四周邊緣
　　　　　鑲嵌骨片，其中七面邊框鏤有扁圓形窗孔，各裝一對銅製小鈸，一面
　　　　　邊框裝有小銅環，繫兩根絲穗。面徑 16.5 厘米、框高 5.5 厘米。

演奏方法：左手持鼓，鼓身豎置，右手敲擊鼓面發聲，有坐、彈、墊、輪等技巧。
　　　　　或搖振鼓身，以小鈸互擊發聲。

功能：主要用於單弦等說唱伴奏，白族用以伴奏歌舞。

Bajiaogu (Eight-cornered drum)

Found among the Han, Manchurians, and the Bai people

Small single-faced eight-sided frame drum with python skin; one side has a short
handle, the other seven sides are each attached a pair of small metallic cymbal.

Played by holding and twisting the drum with the left hand and hitting the drum
surface with right hand

D: 16.5 cm

Used to accompany story singing in North China, and, among the Bai people, to
accompany song and dance performances

47

蜂鼓　又名陶鼓、瓦鼓、橫鼓、花腰鼓

類型：打擊樂器

民族：壯、瑤、毛南等民族。

收藏年代：1997年採集於廣西河池。

樂器說明：活動雙面蜂腰形。一端呈圓球狀，球形直徑28.5厘米，鼓面直徑8厘米，另一端呈喇叭狀，鼓面直徑18厘米。中腰部細而空，形似蜂腰，腰徑9.7厘米。全長52厘米。

演奏方法：將鼓豎向夾於兩腿間敲擊。也可鼓繩掛頸，將鼓橫置身前或置於長架及凳上，立奏、坐奏或邊奏邊舞。

功能：用於節日、喜慶、喪葬和娛樂場所。

Fenggu ("Bee" drum)

Found among the Zhuang, Yao, Maonan and other national minorities

Acquired in Heci of Guangxi province

Hour-glass shaped double-faced drum with a very slender waist, hence the "bee" description

Played by having it squeezed vertically between one's thighs, hung around one's neck, or placed horizontally on a frame or bench

L: 52 cm

Used for festivals, funerary rites, and other entertainment occasions

48

點鼓 又稱懷鼓

類型：打擊樂器

民族：漢族

收藏年代：1958 年

樂器說明：固定雙面框架。鼓身扁圓，鼓框用硬木製作。中間微高，邊緣漸低，
兩面蒙以牛皮，用密排鼓釘繃緊。腔徑 19.5 厘米，高 6.4 厘米。

演奏方法：將鼓的一邊直立於右膝上，鼓的一面向前，右手腕部壓住鼓的上方
邊緣，使之固定同時用右手執鼓槌敲擊。

功能：用於十番鼓器樂合奏或昆曲清唱伴奏。

Huaigu (Lap drum)

Found among the Han people

Double-faced frame drum with leather drum face

Played by vertically resting it on the right knee, slanting slightly forward,
held in place with one's right wrist, and played with a beater with the
right hand

D: 19.5 cm, H: 6.4 cm

Used in the Shifangu ensemble music of Jiangsu province and as
accompaniment to Kunqu singing

49

額 漢族稱手鼓

類型：打擊樂器

民族：藏族、門巴族。

收藏年代：1958年

樂器說明：有柄雙面框架。兩面蒙牛皮，鼓心及四周繪有鮮艷的圖案紋飾。鼓
　　　　　槌用細藤條製成弓形，木製槌柄，握部雕有龍頭。高57.3厘米，面
　　　　　徑 32 厘米，槌長 57.2 厘米。

演奏方法：左手持鼓柄，右手持執弓形鼓槌擊奏發音。因鼓槌落點部位不同，
　　　　　音響隨之變化。

功能：原為藏族宗教樂器。現已成為歌舞演出的主要樂器。多用於熱巴舞等民
　　　間歌舞伴奏。

Shougu (Hand drum)

Found among the Tibetans and Menba people

Double-faced frame drum with a handle and leather drum face; drum
beater is in the shape of a bow

Left hand holds the drum with the handle while right hand beats the
drum face with the beater

D: 32 cm, H: 57.3 cm

Originally used in religious rituals by Tibetans; nowadays used mainly to
accompany secular song and dance performances

50

南音扁鼓 又名餅鼓

類型：打擊樂器

民族：漢族

收藏年代：20世紀50年代

樂器說明：固定雙面框架。面徑17.5厘米、框高5厘米。

演奏方法：左手將鼓持於手上，或捏鼓邊，彎放於肩上，右手執槌敲擊。
在現代南音演唱中，可將扁鼓置於三角竹架上敲擊。

功能：用於福建南音。

***Nanyin biangu* (Flat drum for *Nanyin*)**

Found among the Han people

Double-faced frame drum

Left hand holding the drum frame, sometimes placing it on one's
shoulder or on a bamboo frame; right hand striking it with beater

D: 17.5 cm

Used to accompany *Nanyin* singing of Fujian province

51

撥浪鼓

類型：打擊樂器

民族：漢族

收藏年代：20世紀50年代初

樂器説明：雙面框架搖鼓。面徑14厘米，鼓腔高6厘米，柄長24厘米，柄徑2厘米。

演奏方法：手執鼓柄旋轉搖動，使鼓墜敲擊鼓面發聲。

功能：用於歷代宮廷雅樂，後流傳民間，成為貨郎招攬顧客的訊號。

Bolanggu (Drum)

Found among the Han people

Double-faced frame drum with a long handle and attached beaters on strings

Played by holding the handle and twisting it from side to side

D: 14 cm

Originally used in court ritual music; later among commoners and used as signals by vendors to attract customers

52

細腰陶鼓

類型：打擊樂器

民族：壯族

收藏年代：1958 年

樂器說明：活動雙面沙漏形。兩頭鼓膜上開十五孔，用線連接，居鼓面15厘米處用繩
　　　　　固定，可以調節音高。全長27厘米，面徑 14.5 厘米，腰徑 5 厘米。

演奏方法：雙手拍擊鼓面發聲。

功能：祭祀、歌舞。

Xiyao taogu (Narrow-waisted clay drum)

Found among the Zhuang people

Double-faced hour-glass shaped drum

Played by hitting drum faces with palms

L: 27 cm, D: 14.5 cm

Used in sacrificial ceremonies and song and dance performances

53

瑤族長鼓

類型：打擊樂器

民族：瑤族

收藏年代：1964 年

樂器説明：固定雙面沙漏形。鼓身細長，一端呈喇叭狀，一端呈圓錐狀，形成兩個共
鳴腔。兩端鼓面繪有陰陽魚。全長 68 厘米，腰徑 3.5 厘米，喇叭狀一端面
徑 11 厘米，鼓腔長 29 厘米。圓錐狀一端面徑 6.5 厘米，鼓腔高 28 厘米。

演奏方法：左手執鼓腰，右手拍擊，並隨之轉身舞蹈。

功能：節日及喜慶活動。

Yaozu changgu ("Long" drum of the Yao people)

Found among the Yao people

Double-faced hour-glass shaped drum with a narrow and long mid-section

Played by holding the drum waist with left hand and striking the drum faces
with the right hand as the drummer dances

L: 68 cm

Used mainly in joyous festivities

54

沙鼓 又名饅頭鼓、沙的、和尚頭

類型：打擊樂器

民族：漢族

收藏年代：20 世紀 50 年代初

樂器說明：單面鍋形。鼓框由四塊堅實木料粘合而成。蒙牛皮，鼓心窄小。發音
清脆。通高 11 厘米，鼓心直徑 3.5 厘米，底面直徑 17.5 厘米。

演奏方法：用一根長約 50 厘米的藤條或竹製鼓箭敲擊。

功能：用於粵劇伴奏及佛山"十番鑼鼓"。

Shagu ("Sha" drum)

Found among the Han people

Single-faced bowl-shaped drum with thick buffalo leather as drum surface,
producing a sharp and crisp sound

Played by a bamboo or rattan beater

H: 11 cm

Used in Cantonese opera and the Shifan drum music in Foshan

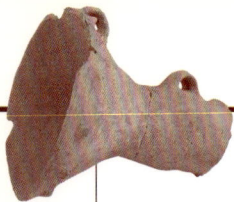

55

狼帳　又名狼鼓、狼唱、蓬蓬鼓

類型：打擊樂器

民族：漢族

收藏年代：20世紀50年代初

樂器說明：雙面活動沙漏狀。鼓身木製，中部細小，兩端大而內空，蒙牛皮。裝有金屬圓環，繫繩索繃帶，全長59.1厘米、兩面鼓腔口徑25.5厘米。

演奏方法：左手握住鼓腰，右手五指並攏，拍擊鼓的正面(是指碗狀口的一端)。

功能：用於閩劇伴奏和民間器樂合奏"籠吹"、"福建十番"、"漳州南詞"的"十全腔"等。

Langgu ("Wolf" drum)

Found among the Han people

Double-faced hour-glass shaped drum with narrow waist, buffalo-leather as drum face

Played by the left hand holding the drum waist with the right hand hitting the drum face

L: 59.1 cm

Used in Fujian opera and various kinds of instrumental ensemble music in the Fujian area

56

秧歌鼓

類型：打擊樂器

民族：漢族

收藏年代：此為傳世品。原為京劇大師程硯秋收藏。並於
　　　　　1958 年捐贈本所。

樂器說明：固定雙面桶形，比腰鼓稍小。鼓身罩以真絲繡花
　　　　　鼓套，其上有鼓帶，下端綴以一排黃色絲穗。
　　　　　鼓身長 33 厘米，面徑 12 厘米。

演奏方法：手持木槌擊奏

功能：用於民間歌舞

Yanggegu ("Rice-planting song" drum)

Found among the Han people
A gift from Cheng Yanqiu
Double-faced barrel-shaped drum
Played by having the drum draped around one's shoulder
and struck with wooden beater
L: 33 cm, D: 12 cm
Used in folk song and dance performances

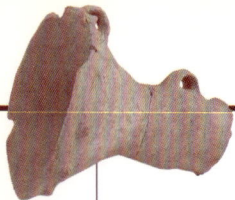

57

花盆鼓　又有南唐鼓、缸鼓之稱

類型：打擊樂器

民族：漢族

收藏年代：1962 年

樂器說明：雙面花盆形。鼓身木製，板材鋸成上寬下窄的鼓梆，堆粘成鼓腔後
　　　　　經車旋而成。兩面蒙皮。鼓身涂深棕色漆，彩繪金龍圖案，帶
　　　　　鼓架。面徑 58 厘米，底面徑 33 厘米，高 63 厘米。

演奏方法：懸於鼓架，用雙木槌敲擊鼓面。

功能：主要用於器樂合奏及民俗活動。

Huapengu ("Flower pot" drum)

Found among the Han people

Double-faced "flower pot"-shaped drum with wooden frame and leather
drum face

Suspended from a frame and struck with two wooden beaters

D: 58 cm, H: 63 cm

Used in instrumental ensemble music and other ritual activities

弦鳴樂器 *CHORDOPHONES*

58

銅琵琶

類型：撥彈樂器

民族：漢族

收藏年代：20世紀50年代

樂器説明：銅製有頸盒形板面類。四相，十二品。缺一弦軸，
以木軸代之。通高100厘米，面寬31.5厘米。

演奏方法：豎抱，五指彈奏。

功能：獨奏、伴奏、合奏。

Tong Pipa (**Copper pear-shaped plucked lute**)
Found among the Han people
Pipa with four triangular bridges along the neck and twelve
frets along the body; missing an original tuning peg
H: 100 cm, W: 31.5 cm
Used for solo and ensemble music, or to accompany singing

59

五弦琵琶 又稱五弦

類型：撥彈樂器

民族：古代北方民族

收藏年代：仿日本奈良正倉院藏品製。原為京劇大師程硯秋
　　　　　舊藏，1953 年捐贈。

樂器說明：木製有頸盒形板面類。項直，無品，通體嵌螺鈿
　　　　　花紋，捍撥處粘玳瑁薄片，其上用螺鈿嵌駱駝載
　　　　　胡人彈琵琶圖象。全長108.5 厘米。

演奏方法：原為橫抱，木撥彈奏。

功能：用於宮廷雅樂。

Wuxian Pipa (Five-stringed pear-shaped plucked lute)

Replica of Tang dynasty instrument in the collection of
Shōsōin in Nara, Japan

Found among the ancient northern people

A gift from Cheng Yanqiu

Played by holding it horizontally and plucked with a
wooden plectrum

L: 108.5 cm

Used for court ritual music

60

清阮

類型：撥彈樂器

民族：漢族等

製作年代：清代 (1644–1911)，梵福樓製。

收藏年代：傳世品。 1958 年汪夢舒捐贈。

樂器說明：木製釘狀盒形板面類。琴首為長矛形。面板刻有款
書。四軫、四弦、八品，相鄰兩弦各為一組，每兩
弦調為同度音。長 117 厘米，音箱直徑 38 厘米。

演奏方法：左手持琴按弦取音，右手用假指甲或執撥片彈奏。

功能：用於宮廷雅樂。

Qing *Ruan* (Long-necked plucked lute)

Made in the Qing dynasty (1644–1911) by Fanfulou
A gift from Wang Mengshu
Wooden body and surface with four tuning pegs, eight
frets, and two sets of double strings; plucked with fingers
or plectrum
L: 117 cm
Used for court ritual music

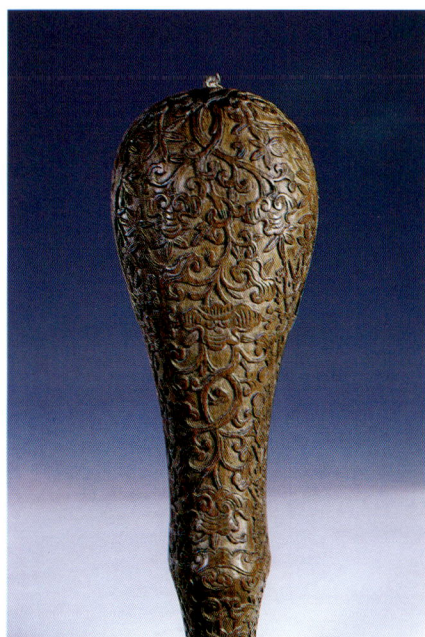

61

火不思 又稱渾不似、琥珀詞、和必斯、吳撥四等

類型：撥彈樂器

民族：蒙古、漢等民族。

製作年代：明代 (1368–1644)

收藏年代：傳世品。本所收藏於 20 世紀 50 年代。

樂器說明：木製直頸碗形皮面類。四軸、四弦、音箱蒙蟒皮，竹碼，背部和弦
軸等部位雕有精美花紋。長 83.5 厘米，面寬 12.5 厘米。

演奏方法：斜抱，右手無名指、小指立於皮面上，主要用拇指、輔以食指挑弦。

功能：彈唱、獨奏、伴奏、合奏。

Huobusi (Four-stringed plucked lute)

Used by Mongolian and Han people

Made in the Ming dynasty (1368–1644)

Straight-neck and bow-shaped body with four strings covered with python skin; plucked with thumb and index finger

L: 83.5 cm, W: 12.5 cm

Used for solo and ensemble music, or to accompany singing

62

忽雷

類型：彈弦樂器

民族：漢族

製作年代：清代 (1644–1911)

收藏年代：傳世品。鄭穎蓀舊藏，本所購於 20 世紀 50 年代。

樂器說明：木製直頸碗形皮面類。琴首為雕刻紅色龍頭，兩側各
　　　　　置一象牙軫，頸細而長，貼象牙板，兩條絲弦由龍口
　　　　　穿出。背鬆犀皮漆，紅色，有片雲、松鱗斑紋。製作
　　　　　精美，工藝考究。通高 86.5 厘米。面寬 18.5 厘米。

演奏方法：抱握撥彈

功能：用於宮廷雅樂。

Hulei (Plucked lute)

Made in the Qing dynasty (1644–1911)

Found among the Han people

Straight-necked and bow-shaped body with two strings

H: 86.5 cm, W: 18.5 cm

Used for court ritual music

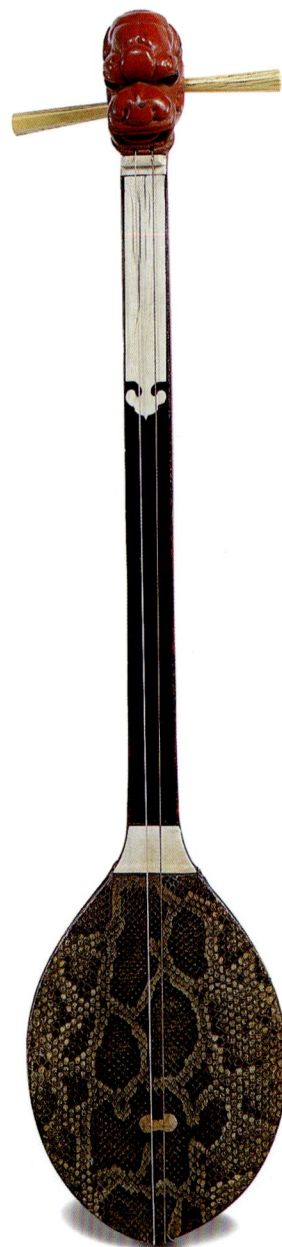

63

小箜篌

類型：撥彈樂器
民族：漢族等
收藏年代：傳世品。鄭穎蓀舊藏，本所購於 20 世紀 50 年代。
樂器說明：木製框架角形。張十三條相同直頸的絲弦。在角形立柱背部雕刻有對
　　　　　稱鳳凰和雲頭、花卉圖飾，並刻有楷書 "欵侯" 二字。通高 80 厘米，
　　　　　底長 23.5 厘米，共鳴槽寬 5.5 厘米。
演奏方法：左手托置，右手彈奏。
功能：古代多用於儀仗樂隊。

Xiao Konghou (Small harp)

Found among the Han and other people
Triangular wooden frame with 13 silk strings
Held in left hand and plucked by right hand
H: 80 cm
Used in ritual procession music

64

箜篌

類型：撥彈樂器

民族：漢族等

收藏年代：仿古製品。原為京劇大師程硯秋舊藏，1953 年
捐贈本所。

樂器說明：木製框架角形。通體鬆紅漆，描繪金色龍紋。
高 137 厘米，座寬 47.5 厘米。二十三弦。

演奏方法：豎抱於怀中，用兩手齊奏。

功能：用於宮廷雅樂。

Konghou (**Harp**)

Modern replica of ancient sample

Found among the Han and other people

A gift from Cheng Yanqiu

Held in lap and played by both hands

H: 137 cm

Used in court ritual music

65

瑟

類型：撥彈樂器

民族：漢族

製作年代：清咸豐七年 (1857)，傳世品。

收藏年代：原為京劇大師梅蘭芳舊藏，1953 年捐贈本所。

樂器説明：木製半管狀板面類。二十五弦。琴面繪有精美彩色二龍戲珠及花紋圖案，
琴框刻有"置"字樣。全長 211 厘米，頭寬 47 厘米，尾寬 39.3 厘米。

演奏方法：平置，左手按弦，右手彈撥發聲。

功能：用於歌唱伴奏，同時用於宮廷雅樂及丁祭活動。

Se (Bridged plucked zither)

Made in 7th year of Xianfeng period (1857) of Qing dynasty

A gift from Mei Lanfang

Found among the Han people

L: 211 cm

Wooden half-tube long zither with 25 strings

Used for court and Confucian sacrificial rituals, and to accomopany singing

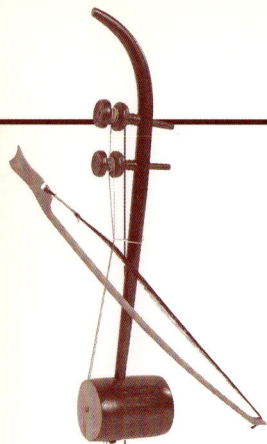

66

五弦琴　又稱均鐘

民族：漢族等

製作年代：湖北曾候乙墓葬出土文物複製品，原件藏湖北省博物館。

樂器說明：木製棒狀板面類。器身用獨木斫成，中空，構成音箱。尾部為實體。首端
　　　　近方，立一蘑菇狀柱，柱高4.4厘米，供拴弦之用；尾端近圓。首、尾各
　　　　岳山。兩岳間距(隱間)106厘米。兩岳外側，均並列5個弦孔，孔徑0.3
　　　　厘米，孔距約為1厘米通體以黑漆為底，除音箱面板部分外，均以朱、黃
　　　　兩色相間遍飾精細絢麗的紋樣。全長115厘米，首寬7厘米，高4厘米；
　　　　尾寬5.5厘米，高1.4厘米。

功能：據考，此器至遲於公元前6世紀已在周王宮廷內使用，並似在秦、漢時失傳的
　　　均鐘——一種為編鐘調律的音高標准器(《國語》)。

Wuxianqin (Five-stringed plucked zither)

Replica of the sample discovered in the tomb of Marquis Yi of Zeng,
ca. 433 BC

Rod-shaped hollow wooden box with five string holes

L: 115 cm

Used as tuning standard for bell chimes in Pre-Qin times

67

唱詞琴　又名牛筋琴

類型：擊弦樂器

民族：漢族

收藏年代：1959 年

樂器說明：木製平板盒狀板面類。面板桐木製，兩端有岳山，張十二條牛筋弦，琴底
　　　　　一端設機械螺旋裝置，用以繃緊調整粗硬的琴弦。底板下開兩銅錢幣形音
　　　　　孔。弦下施柱，一弦一柱。長 51.1 厘米，寬 27.3 厘米，高 5.7 厘米。

演奏方法：演唱者左手執拍板，右手以小棍敲琴，兼擊扁鼓。發音淳樸渾厚，別具地
　　　　　方色彩。

功能：流行於浙江南部的瑞安、平陽、溫州、永加等地。是溫州鼓詞的伴奏樂器。

Changci Qin (Zither to accompany poetry) or *Niujing Qin* (Buffalo-gut zither)

Found among the Han people

Twelve buffalo gut strings stretched lengthwise along a rectangular wooden box, each string over a bridge

Played by striking the strings with a small stick

L: 51.1 cm, W: 27.3 cm, H: 5.7 cm

Used to accompany drumsongs in southern Zhejiang province

68

揚琴　又稱洋琴、打琴、銅絲琴、扇面琴、蝙蝠琴、蝴蝶琴

類型：擊弦樂器

民族：漢、蒙古等民族。

收藏年代：20 世紀 50 年代

樂器說明：木製平板盒狀板面類。音箱呈蝴蝶狀。音箱內對應面板琴碼上膠有音梁，張鋼絲弦，
　　　　　高音用裸弦，低音用纏弦。琴籤竹製。琴長 79 厘米，寬 34 厘米，高 5.8 厘米。

演奏方法：置琴於架，左右手各執一琴竹直接擊奏條碼兩側之弦。

功能：用於廣東音樂、江南絲竹、揚州清音、二人台等樂種、曲種。

Yangqin (Dulcimer)

Found among the Han and Mongolian people

A large number of metal strings stretched over a wooden soundbox in the shape of a stretched butterfly wings, each over a low bridge

Played with two bamboo beaters

L: 79 cm, W: 34 cm, H: 5.8 cm

Used for instrumental ensemble music and accompanying singing in Guangdong, Jiangnan area, and northern China

69

清琵琶

類型：撥彈樂器

民族：漢族

製作年代：清代 (1644–1911)，傳世品。

樂器說明：木製有頸盒形板面類。四相，十二品。琴背部有
　　　　　 "鳴玉" 二字，旁刻 "妙嚴居士寅生氏題篆" 並
　　　　　 "寅生" 方印。通高 91 厘米，面寬 25.4 厘米。

演奏方法：豎抱，五指彈奏。左手有揉、吟、帶起、捺打、
　　　　　 虛按、絞弦、泛音、推、挽、綽、注等指法；右
　　　　　 手有彈、挑、滾、勾、抹、拂、掃、輪等指法。

功能：獨奏、伴奏、合奏。

Qing *Pipa* (Qing-dynasty plucked lute)

Found among the Han people

Made in the Qing dynasty (1644–1911)

Wooden lute with pear-shaped body and four strings, four
triangular bridges along the neck and twelve frets along
the body

Played by holding the instrument vertically in one's lap,
with left hand fingers stopping the strings and right hand
fingers plucking

H: 91 cm, W: 25.4 cm

Used for solo and ensemble music and as accompaniment
to singing

古樂風流

70

八角琴

類型：撥彈樂器

民族：漢族

收藏年代：1963 年

樂器説明：木製釘狀盒形板面類。音箱成八方形，形似雙清，每個框邊都鑲嵌精細的山水人物雕刻。兩軸張兩弦，軸定雕刻梅花，設十二個品位。全長89厘米，音箱對邊距離26厘米，厚5厘米。

演奏方法：琴鼓置於右腿上，琴頭斜向左上方，左手按弦，右手用撥子彈奏。

功能：流行於福建莆田、仙游等地，在民間器樂樂種"十音"、"八樂"中使用，後也用於莆仙戲伴奏。

Bajiao Qin (Eight-cornered plucked lute)

Found among the Han people

A lute-type instrument with an eight-sided box as resonance chamber, two strings, and twelve frets

Played by holding the instrument vertically but slightly slanted to the left, left hand fingers stopping the string, right hand plucking the string with a plectrum

L: 89 cm

Used for instrumental ensemble music and opera in various regions of Fujian province

71

秦琴

類型：撥彈樂器

民族：漢族

收藏年代：20 世紀 60 年代初

樂器說明：木製釘狀盒形板面類。琴杆窄而長，用柴木製作。三弦十二品。音箱由六塊硬木板膠接而成，呈梅花狀，兩面蒙桐木面板。全長 90 厘米、音箱直徑 27 厘米、厚 5.3 厘米。

演奏方法：左手持琴，右手用撥子彈奏。

功能：原只用於廣東音樂，現已廣泛用於地方戲劇伴奏、民族樂隊。

Qin *Qin* (Qin plucked lute)

Found among the Han people

Wooden box-shaped body in the shape of a plum flower with a long neck; 3 strings and 12 frets; plucked with plectrum

L: 90 cm

Originally used in Cantonese instrumental ensemble music; now widely used in many regional operas and orchestras

72

雙清

類型：撥彈樂器

民族：漢族

收藏年代：20 世紀 50 年代初

樂器説明：木製釘狀盒形板面類。八方形音箱，軫、品、岳山
　　　　　縛弦均為象牙製，四弦十四品。通高99厘米，面
　　　　　寬22厘米。

演奏方法：左手持琴，右手用撥子彈奏。

功能：用於器樂合奏、戲曲伴奏及"憎"、"八樂"等樂種。

Shuangqing **("Shuangqing" plucked lute)**
Found among the Han people
Wooden eight-sided sound box with four strings and
14 frets
H: 99 cm, W: 22 cm
Plucked with plectrum
Used in opera and instrumental ensemble music

73

柳琴　又名柳葉琴

類型：撥彈樂器

民族：漢族

收藏年代：20世紀60年代初

樂器說明：木製有頸盒形板面類。三弦，二十四品。如意琴
　　　　　頭，黃楊木軸，竹製山口、品，紅木縛弦，黑色
　　　　　漆，通高66厘米。桐木面板，寬21厘米。

演奏方法：琴斜置胸前。左手持琴按弦，右手執撥彈奏。右
　　　　　手技巧有彈、挑、雙彈、雙挑、掃、拂等，左手
　　　　　有吟弦、打弦、帶弦、推拉弦等。

功能：魯南、蘇北一帶柳琴戲、安徽泗州戲的主奏樂器。
　　　現也用於獨奏及民間器樂合奏。

Liu Qin ("Willow leaf" plucked lute)

Found among the Han people

Wooden soundbox with short neck, three strings and
24 frets

Plucked with plectrum

H: 66 cm

Used in regional operas of southern Shandong, northern
Jiangsu, and Anhui, and as solo and instrumental
ensemble music

74

玎膽 又名森(傣)、馬腿琴(阿昌、德昂)

類型：撥彈樂器

民族：傣族、阿昌族、德昂族

收藏年代：20世紀50年代末

樂器說明：木製有頸盒形板面類。無品位，設三軸，張鋼絲弦。琴頭雕刻一孔雀為飾。正面下半部蒙長17.5、寬5厘米的松木板，一側距底端5厘米處開一音孔。琴身全長54厘米。

演奏方法：將琴置於兩腿間，琴身向前，稍傾斜，或橫抱於胸前。左手扶琴頸按弦，右手食指綁一骨片、竹片或削尖的雞羽管為撥子，在音孔下方彈奏。

功能：用於獨奏或為民歌、說唱伴奏，也用於青年男女愛情生活。

Dingdan ("Dingdan" plucked lute)

Found among the Tai and other people

Wooden lute-type instrument with three metal strings but no frets

Plucked with a plectrum made of bamboo, animal bone, or chicken feather

L: 54 cm

Used for solo performance and to accompany singing and narrative songs, and for courtship

75

冬不拉

類型：撥彈樂器

民族：哈薩克族

收藏年代：1963 年

樂器說明：木製有頸盒形板面類，音箱瓢形，由七塊核桃木拼合
而成。琴杆上貼塑料指板，粘19道塑料品，竹碼，張
兩弦。松木面板，上開一圓形音孔，寬 22.7 厘米，
通高 95 厘米。

演奏方法：左手持琴，右手撥奏。

功能：用於 "阿肯" 彈唱，也用於獨奏和合奏。

Dongbula ("Dongbula" plucked lute)

Found among the Hasak people

Wooden lute-type instrument with 2 strings

Plucked with fingers

H: 95 cm, W: 22.7 cm

Used for solo and ensemble music and to accompany singing

76

彈不爾

類型：撥彈樂器

民族：維吾爾族、烏孜別克族。

收藏年代：1959 年

樂器説明：木製直頸碗形板面類。音箱較小，上置兩個竹製
高音品和兩個小音孔。琴頸細長，絲弦纏成 25
個品位，琴頭平頂無飾，上置五個 "T" 形弦軸，
張五根鋼絲弦。全長 123 厘米。

演奏方法：共鳴箱斜置於右腿根部，左手扶杆按弦，右手食
指套鋼絲撥或執牛角、塑料撥片彈奏。右手有
彈、強彈、撥、雙彈、滾、琵彈等技法，左手有
滑音、顫音。打音、泛音、揉音等技法。

功能：用於獨奏、伴奏和器樂合奏。

Tanbu'er ("Tanbu'er" plucked lute)

Found among Uighur and Uzbek people

Wooden lute-type instrument with a small bowl-shaped
sound box, five metal strings and 25 frets

Plucked by either plastic or buffalo bone plectrum or
by metal thimbles

L: 123 cm

Used for solo and ensemble music and for accompaniment to singing

都它爾

類型：撥彈樂器

民族：維吾爾族、烏孜別克族。

收藏年代：1959 年

樂器說明：木製直頸碗形板面類。琴杆細長，紅木指板，上
　　　　　鑲嵌骨飾，纏有十九道絲弦品。竹碼，張兩弦。
　　　　　音箱背面嵌九條骨飾瓣紋，面寬17.5厘米，通高
　　　　　125 厘米。

演奏方法：演奏採用坐姿，左手扶琴按弦，拇指按里弦，食
　　　　　指按外弦，右手用五指撥彈。左手技巧有揉弦、
　　　　　打弦、叩弦、滑弦等。右手有擊弦、滾彈、斷
　　　　　音、勾弦等技法。

功能：常用於自彈自唱或器樂合奏。

Dutai'er ("Dutai'er" plucked lute)

Found among Uighur and Uzbek people

Wooden lute-type instrument with a bowl-shaped sound
box, two strings and 19 frets

Plucked with right hand fingers

H: 125 cm, W: 17.5 cm

Used for ensemble music or accompany singing

古樂風流

78

熱瓦甫　又名拉瓦波、喇巴卜

類型：撥彈樂器

民族：維吾爾族、烏孜別克族

收藏年代：1958 年

樂器說明：木製直頸碗形皮面類。琴桿較短，上粘指板，鑲黑、白相間骨飾圖
案，嵌二十四個銅製品位，張銅絲弦。音箱較大，採用八塊木板拼
合，蒙蟒皮，琴桿連接處兩側各設一彎角。全長 93 厘米、面寬 12
厘米、厚 12 厘米。

演奏方法：琴平橫於胸前，左手扶琴桿，食指、中指、無名指按弦；右手肘部
夾持琴箱，手指執撥彈奏。

功能：獨奏、合奏及伴奏。

Rewapu ("Rewapu" plucked lute)

Found among the Uighur and Uzbek people

Wooden lute-type instrument with a bowl-shaped sound box covered with
leather, metal strings and 24 frets

Plucked with fingers

L: 93 cm

Used for solo and ensemble music and for accompaniment of singing

79

莆田小三弦

類型：撥彈樂器

民族：漢族

收藏年代：20 世紀 50 年代初

樂器說明：木製釘狀碗形皮面類。琴鼓框呈八方形，每一框
邊均鑲嵌精細的山水人物雕刻，兩面蒙蟒皮，內
堂較小。三軸，一軸雕喜鵲登枝，一軸雕壽桃，
一軸雕打鼓的樂伎。張三條絲弦。後卷書琴頭。
全長 85 厘米，琴鼓長 16 厘米，寬 15 厘米。

演奏方法：左手持琴，右手撥奏。

功能：用於民間器樂樂種 "十音"、"八樂"，也用於莆仙
戲伴奏。

Putian Xiaosanxian (Small sanxian of Putian)

Found among the Han people

Wooden lute-type instrument with python skin for surface of the octagonal, bowl-shaped sound box, three silk strings, no frets

Plucked with fingers

L: 85 cm

Used for instrumental ensemble music and as accompaniment to Puxian opera

80

奚琴 又稱胡琴、鄉胡

類型：擦弦樂器

民族：朝鮮族

收藏年代：1959 年

樂器說明：木製釘狀管形板面類。琴頭呈彎月形，無飾。兩軸置於琴杆上部右側、與琴筒呈平行，軸頂旋成葫蘆形。張兩條老弦。通高 60 厘米，筒長 12.4 厘米，筒前口 8.3 x 9.5 厘米。

演奏方法：左手扶持琴杆、滿手握弦、不換把位，右手執馬尾弓夾於兩弦間擦奏。

功能：是朝鮮族民族樂隊的主奏樂器。

Xi Qin (Bowed lute)

Found among the Chaoxian (Korean) people

Wooden lute-type instrument, cylindrical sound box, two strings, no frets

Bowed with horse-tail bow caught between the two strings

H: 60 cm

Used as principal instrument in the Chaoxian instrumental ensemble

銅筒四胡　又名四弦、二夾弦

類型：擦弦樂器

民族：蒙古族

收藏年代：1958 年

樂器說明：銅、木製釘狀管形皮面類。琴杆略長而粗，置四
　　　　　軸，張四弦。琴筒由 0.1 厘米厚黃銅板卷製，琴
　　　　　筒前後加筒箍。麻花形弦軸，軸頂鑲骨飾。通高
　　　　　83.5 厘米，琴頭方形，平頂嵌骨飾，筒長 13.6
　　　　　厘米，前口徑 8.5 厘米，弓長 78 厘米。

演奏方法：馬尾弓分兩股分別夾於一、二弦和三、四弦之
　　　　　間，演奏時同時擦兩弦發聲。

功能：流行於內蒙古、東北和華北各省、區。是京韻大鼓、
　　　西河大鼓、天津時調、湖北小曲蒙古說書以及二人
　　　台、曲劇、皮影等戲曲的伴奏樂器。

Tongtong Sihu (Four-stringed bowed lute)

Found among the Mongolian people

Lute-type instrument with cylindrical sound box made
of wood and copper with leather surface, four strings,
4 frets

Bowed with a horse-tail bow that is divided into two
strands: one caught between strings one and two, the
other between strings three and four; two-tone intervals
may be produced

H: 83.5 cm

Used in North-eastern provinces, Inner Mongolia, and
other northern provinces, to accompany various kinds
of narrative songs, operas and shadow theaters

古樂風流

82

提琴

類型：擦弦樂器

民族：漢族

製作年代：清代 (1644–1911)，傳世品。

收藏年代：原為著名琵琶演奏家楊大均舊藏，1960 年代捐
贈本所。

樂器說明：木製釘狀碗形板面類。琴筒用椰殼製成，貼以薄
桐木面板。琴頭鑲嵌象牙雕花，一側置兩軸，各
繫絲弦一條，經面板上的琴碼固定於琴筒下端。
不設千斤。從琴杆上端山口處開始即可按弦演
奏。琴筒下安支柱，琴弓為竹製，上張馬尾。全
長 98.8 厘米。

演奏方法：兩腿夾持，以保持琴體的穩定。左手持琴，右手
持弓擦奏。

功能：用於崑曲清唱和器樂合奏。蘇州玄妙道教樂隊中也使
用提琴。

Ti Qin (Bowed lute)

Found among the Han people

Made in the Qing dynasty (1644–1911)

A gift from Yang Dajun

Wooden lute-type, coconut shell soundbox with board
surface, two silk strings, bamboo bow with horse tail

Played by having sound box squeezed between thighs

L: 98.8 cm

Used in Kunqu opera and instrumental ensemble music

83

馬頭琴

類型：擦弦樂器

民族：蒙古族

製作年代：清代 (1644–1911)

樂器說明：木製釘狀盒形皮面類。琴頭雕刻馬頭為飾，琴杆上部左右各置一弦軸，張兩條馬尾弦。框板為硬木製，音箱呈正梯形，兩面蒙皮，描繪彩色圖案，琴箱背面開一金錢狀音孔。琴弓用藤條作杆，拴以馬尾，弓長75.5厘米。通高105.7厘米。音箱高9.4厘米，上寬23厘米，下寬26厘米。

演奏方法：坐奏，音箱夾於兩腿中間，琴杆偏向左側。左手持琴按弦，右手執馬尾弓在弦外擦奏。按弦法頗為獨特，食指和中指伸入弦下用指甲頂弦，無名指用指尖按弦，小指用指尖頂弦。有顫指、滑音、雙音、撥弦、揉弦、泛音等技巧。右手有頓弓、擊弓、碎弓、抖弓、跳弓等技巧。

功能：明清時用於宮廷樂隊，現除獨奏外，並用於民歌、說書的伴奏，亦常與四胡等樂器合奏。

Matou Qin ("Horse's Head" bowed lute)

Found among the Mongolian people

Made in the Qing dynasty (1644–1911)

Wooden lute-type with box-shaped sound box of leather surface, horse's head carving at tip of long neck, two strings of horse tail hair, bow of horse tail hair

Played by having sound box placed in between the thighs

H: 105.7 cm

Used in court orchestra during Ming and Qing dynasties, as solo and accompaniment to folksongs and narrative songs today

84

京二胡　原稱甕子

類型：擦弦樂器

民族：漢族

收藏年代：20 世紀 60 年代初

樂器説明：木製釘狀管形皮面類。結構形製略小於二胡。琴
　　　　　頭呈方形，平頂無飾，稍向後彎曲。兩軸兩弦，
　　　　　設千斤，置琴碼。琴筒呈六角形，後口加邊框，
　　　　　長 11.7 厘米，前口對邊長 5 厘米。琴杆長 55.2
　　　　　厘米。弓長 72 厘米。

演奏方法：左手執琴杆按弦，右手執弓擦奏。

功能：20 世紀 20 年代，由京胡演奏家王少卿首次用於京劇
　　　唱腔伴奏。現也用於川劇、豫劇、評劇伴奏。

Jing Erhu (Bowed lute for Peking opera)

Found among the Han people

Wooden lute-type instrument with hexagonal cross-section cylindrical sound box, two strings with a bow of horse tail caught between them

L: 67 cm

First used as accompaniment to Peking opera in the 1920s by Wang Shaoqing, now also used in Sichuan, Henan, and North-eastern operas

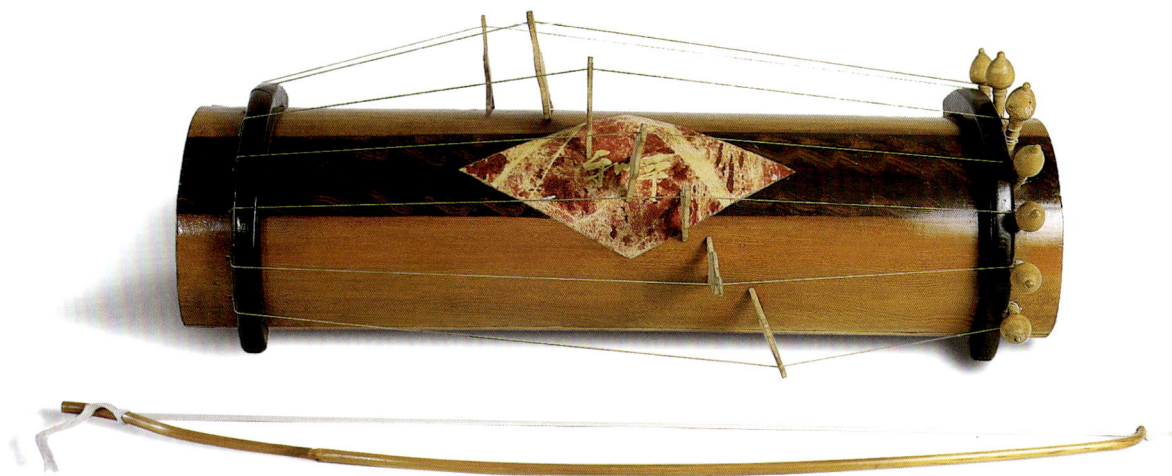

85

箏尼　又名瓦琴、唐琴、福琴、梧桐琴、七弦琴

類型：擦弦樂器

民族：壯族

收藏年代：20世紀60年代

樂器說明：木製半管狀板面類。取材泡桐，張七條絲弦，弦下施柱，柱用李子
　　　　　木製作。槽的一端設有七軸，軸用柚木製。琴身下有杉木底板。用
　　　　　馬尾弓擦奏，弓杆用竹片削製。全長60厘米，寬16.5厘米。

演奏方法：用左手持琴橫於胸前，右手握弓擦弦，轉動琴體與運弓配合。全用
　　　　　空弦音，偶有撥弦。

功能：用於節日喜慶、婚嫁迎娶及工休娛樂。

Zhengni (Bowed zither)

Found among the Zhuang people

Wooden half tube long zither, seven silk strings each over a bridge, horse tail bow; strings are bowed but occasionally plucked

Played by having the instrument held vertically in front so that it can be rotated for the bow to reach all strings

L: 60 cm, W: 16.5 cm

Used in festivals, weddings, and other leisurely occasions

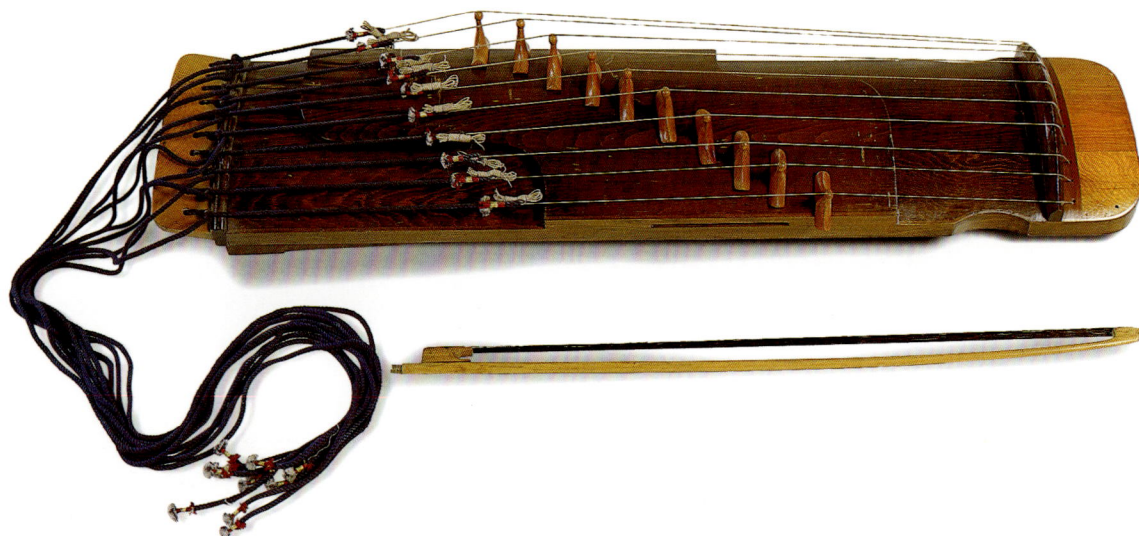

86

牙箏

類型：擦弦樂器

民族：朝鮮族

收藏年代：1959 年

樂器説明：木製半管狀板面類。張十弦，一弦一柱 (碼)。絲弦繫於琴端弦孔内，
弦尾繫木棉繩，松緊染尾可調節音高。底板開有一長方形出音孔。全
長 102.7 厘米，首寬 11.5 厘米，尾寬 22 厘米。

演奏方法：右端置於案上，左端著地。左手用拇指、食指、中指、無名指按弦。
右手執竹或馬尾弓擦奏。

功能：用於民間器樂合奏和伴奏。尤適於演奏朝鮮族民間音樂散曲和古曲等。

Yazheng (Bowed zither)

Found among the Chaoxian (Korean) people

Wooden half tube long zither, ten silk strings each over a bridge, bamboo
or horse tail bow

Played by having the left end on a low table and right end on ground, left
hand fingers stopping string, right hand bowing

L: 102.7 cm

Used for instrumental ensemble music among the Chaoxian people

87

軋琴　又名軋箏琴

類型：擦弦樂器

民族：漢族

收藏年代：1964 年

樂器說明：木製半管狀板面類。面板和底板均用桐木，面板近兩端處有"梁"，
　　　　　即弦枕。張弦十條，弦下施柱，柱用棗木。全長56.2厘米，寬13.1厘
　　　　　米，邊板高 6.3 厘米，兩梁之間距離 36.8 厘米。

演奏方法：左手握琴的一側，將琴舉起，右手持弓橫壓於弦上，兩手同時動作，
　　　　　擦奏琴弦。

功能：流行於河北、邯鄲以及豫北、晉東南等地區，是地方戲曲武安平調的伴奏
　　　樂器。

Ya Qin (Bowed zither)

Found among the Han people

Wooden half tube long zither, ten strings, each over a bridge

Left hand held up one end of instrument, right hand bow the strings

L: 56.2 cm, W: 13.1 cm

Used in regional operas in Hebei, northern Henan, and South-eastern Shanxi

88

十三弦箏

類型：撥彈樂器

民族：漢族

收藏年代：原為京劇大師程硯秋舊藏，1958年捐贈本所。

樂器說明：木製半管狀板面類。琴頭向下傾斜，為中空共鳴體。琴面張十三條
絲弦。通體髹紅色，描繪八寶花紋。全長134厘米、寬20.5厘米。

演奏方法：左手按弦，右手彈撥。

功能：用於器樂獨奏、合奏。

Shisanxian Zheng (Thirteen-string plucked zither)

Found among the Han people

A gift from Cheng Yanqiu

Wooden half tube long zither, thirteen silk strings, each over a bridge

Left hand manipulates string, right hand fingers pluck strings

L: 134 cm, W: 20.5 cm

Used for solo and ensemble music, and as accompaniment to songs and
other solo instruments

89

十六弦箏

類型：撥彈樂器

民族：漢族

收藏年代：20 世紀 50 年代初

樂器說明：木製半管狀板面類。琴頭向下傾斜，為中空共鳴體。裡面膠有音梁，底部開出音孔。首尾部鑲有岳山，琴面置十六條絲弦，設有弦軸、弦柱。框板頂部、底部鑲嵌兩條對稱的白色三角形連接飾紋。全長164 厘米、寬 27 厘米。

演奏方法：左手按弦，右手彈撥。右手可用大指、食指、中指三指，有肉甲撥弦和義甲彈弦之分；左手用食指、中指或中指、無名指捺弦以取"按、顫、揉、推"的變化音。

功能：用於器樂獨奏、伴奏與合奏。

Shiliuxian Zheng (Sixteen-string plucked zither)

Found among the Han people

Wooden half tube long zither, sixteen silk strings, each over a bridge

Left hand manipulates string, right hand fingers pluck strings

L: 164 cm, W: 27 cm

Used as solo and ensemble music, and as accompaniment to songs and other solo instruments

古樂風流

90

伽倻琴

類型：撥彈樂器

民族：朝鮮族

收藏年代：1958 年

樂器說明：木製半管狀板面類。由琴框、面板、底板構成長形音箱。張十三弦，
　　　　　弦下施柱。全長 144.7 厘米，寬 25.5 厘米。

演奏方法：將琴置於桌上或尾端置於地上、首端放在右膝上，右手除小指外均用於
　　　　　彈奏，技巧有彈、撥、滾、琶等，左手技巧有按、顫、推、揉等。

功能：用於伽倻琴彈唱或歌舞伴奏。

Jiaye Qin ("Jiaye" zither, or Kayagum)

Found among the Chaoxian (Korean) people

Wooden half tube long zither, thirteen strings, each over a bridge

Played by placing the zither on a table, or by having the left end on one's
knee and right end on ground

L: 144.7 cm, W: 25.5 cm

Used as solo or accompaniment to singing and dancing

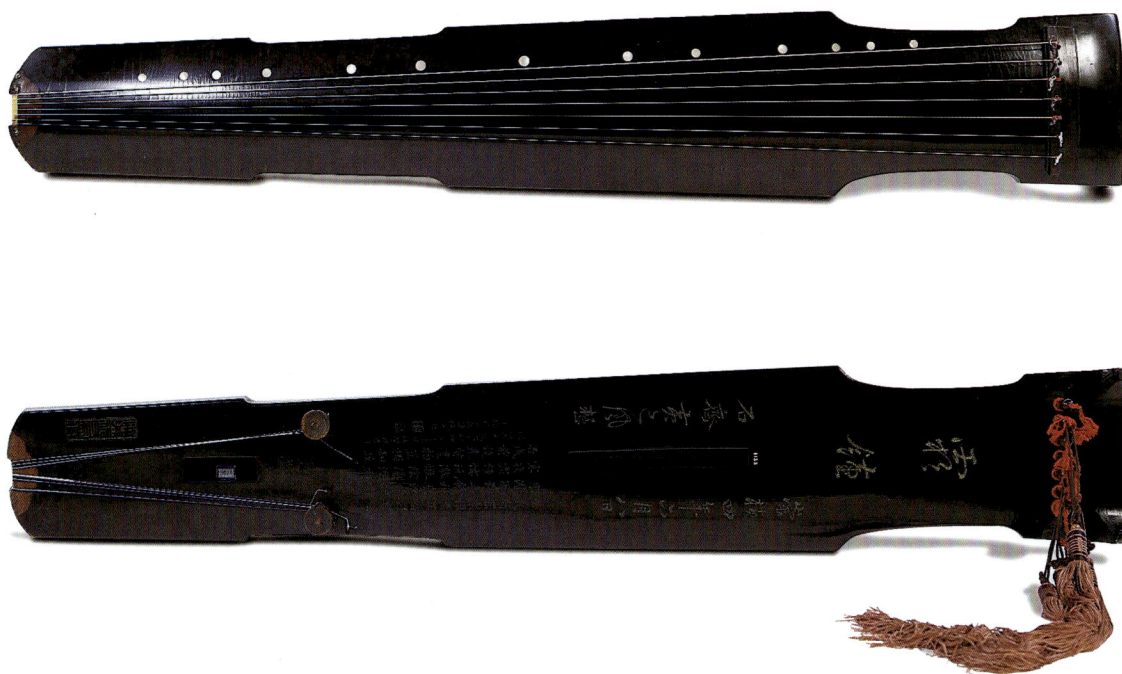

91

古琴 (霜鐘)

長 124 厘米，寬 (額 19 厘米，肩 20 厘米，尾 13 厘米)，厚 5 厘米。

民族：漢族

製作年代：明代，1631 年

漆色斷紋：通體鬆黑色漆，呈小蛇腹斷紋。

琴材配件：紅木軫，紅木雁足。

琴背銘文：(一) 龍池上方刻草書 "霜鐘" 二字。

　　　　　(二) 龍池右側刻 "崇禎四年六月八日"。

　　　　　(三) 龍池左側刻 "石齋黃已風整"。

　　　　　(四) 龍池下刻楷書題識四十八字，落款 "同治六年歲次丁卯仲呂月，漁梁後學祝慶年重修於古無諸城並銘" 二十七字，其下有篆書印二方。

　　　　　(五) 鳳沼上方刻篆書 "心田撒掃淨無塵" 一長方印。

　　　　　(六) 鳳沼下琴尾右刻篆書 "十二琴樓第二才" 七字；琴尾左刻篆書 "浦城祝氏家藏" 六字長方印。

流傳概略：此琴製於 1631 年，1867 年福建莆城清代琴家祝桐君重修並題刻銘文。曾由福建琴家王介眉珍藏。

製作特點：仲尼式，杉木製，龍池、鳳沼均為長方形，納音較高。琴體圓渾寬宏，琴面微弧。

演奏方法：將琴置於桌上。左手用大指、食指、中指、無名指按弦，右手用大指、食指、中指、無名指彈奏。
　　　　　左手有吟、猱、綽、注等技法，右手有勾、剔、抹、挑等技法。

功能：主要用於自娛自樂，古代也用於宮廷雅樂、燕樂及祭祀。

Guqin "Shuangzhong" (*Qin* with name of "Frosted Bell")

Made in 1631, Ming dynasty

L: 124 cm, T: 5 cm

Zhongni (Confucian) style of design

Black lacquer, with fine "snake belly" crack patterns

Various inscriptions, including its name Frosted Bell, and one by Zhu Qingnian in 1867 who repaired the instrument

92

古琴 (鳴鳳)

琴長 126.5 厘米，寬 (額 24 厘米，肩 22.7 厘米，尾 16 厘米) ，
厚 6.5 厘米，有效弦長 115.0 厘米。

民族：漢族

製作年代：南宋 (1127–1279)

漆色斷紋：通體鬆栗殼色漆，後朱漆修補，鹿角灰胎較薄，底有八寶
　　　　　灰修補。琴面呈大小蛇腹間牛毛、小冰裂斷紋，琴底斷
　　　　　紋不甚規則。

琴材配件：木軫，玉雁足，紅木岳山，月白鈞窯瓷徽。

琴背銘文：(一) 龍池上方刻楷書 "鳴鳳"。
　　　　　(二) 龍池兩旁刻行書銘文 "朝陽即昇，巢鳳有聲。朱絲
　　　　　　　　一奏，天下聞名。" 四句。
　　　　　(三) 池下近足處刻外圓內方印，雙鉤篆文 "中和之氣"
　　　　　　　　四字。

製作特點：連珠式變體。桐木製，造型端莊渾厚，面寬而扁，項、腰
　　　　　作連續四弧龍池與鳳沼作三連弧形。池內納音微隆，琴
　　　　　首正面鑲嵌橢圓形玉雕 "翔鳳" 為飾。

Guqin "Mingfeng" (*Qin* with name of "Cry of Phoenix")

Made in the Southern Song dynasty (1127–1279)
L: 126.5 cm, T: 6.5 cm
Variant of Lianzhu ("string of pearl") style of design
Chestnut color lacquer, repaired later with red lacquer. Top surface has large and fine "snake belly" crack patterns mixed with "bovine hair" and fine "cracked ice"; bottom surface with irregular crack patterns.
Various inscriptions, including its name Cry of Phoenix and one that reads "Morning sun about to rise, a sound emerge from the phoenix nest; when the red strings intone, it will be heard all under heaven"

93

古琴 (紅輕雷)

通長 119 厘米，寬 (額 24 厘米，肩 19.5 厘米，尾 14.5 厘米)，厚 5.8 厘米。

民族：漢族

製作年代：南宋 (1127–1279)

漆色斷紋：黑紅色漆，小蛇腹斷，鹿角灰胎。

琴材配件：木軫，木雁足。

琴背銘文：(一) 龍池上方刻篆書 "輕雷" 二字。

(二) 龍池兩旁刻草書銘文："振萬物乎虺虺，獨纖塵乎霏霏。無妄飛而無折摧，是之謂天隨"。

(三) 池內刻 "大唐開元三年雷氏造" 偽託銘文。

製作特點：伏羲式變體，桐木製。琴體圓中帶扁，圓形龍池、鳳沼，納音亦呈圓形，微微隆起。

Guqin "Hong Qing Lei" (*Qin* with name of "Red Soft Thunder")

Made in the Southern Song dynasty (1127–1279)

L: 119 cm, T: 5.8 cm

Variant of Fuxi style of design

Black and red lacquer, fine "snake belly" crack patterns

Various inscriptions, including its name Red Soft Thunder and a forged inscription that reads "made by Master Lei in the third year of the reign Kaiyuan of Tang dynasty"

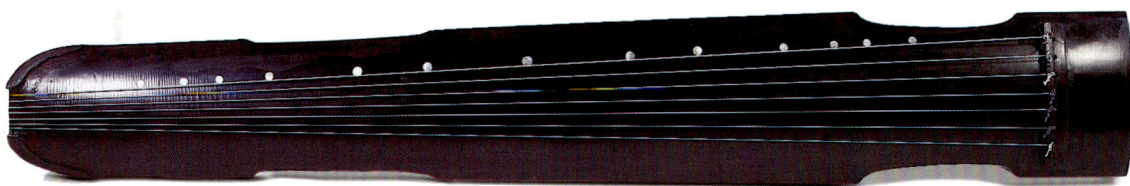

94

古琴 (雪江濤)

長 128.6 厘米，寬 (額 19.6 厘米，肩 19 厘米，尾 12 厘米)，厚 5 厘米。

民族：漢族

製作年代：明代 (1368–1644)

漆色斷紋：鹿角灰胎，胎較薄，表面髹黑漆，呈小蛇腹間流水斷。

琴材配件：木軫，木雁足。

琴背銘文：龍池上方刻有隸書 "雪江濤" 三字，內填金漆。

製作特點：仲尼式，肩在二徽餘處，桐木製。龍池、鳳沼均為長方形。池內納音呈脊狀。

Guqin "Xue Jiang Tao" (*Qin* with name of "Snow River Tide")

Made in the Ming dynasty (1368–1644)

L: 128.6 cm, T: 5 cm

Zhongni (Confucian) style of design

Black lacquer, with fine "snake belly" and "water ripple" crack patterns

Inscription of its name Snow River Tide

95

古琴 (萬壑松風)

長 123.5 厘米，寬 (額 18 厘米，肩 19.3 厘米，尾 14.7 厘米)，厚 4.7 厘米。

民族：漢族

製作年代：明代 (1368–1644)

漆色斷紋：糅栗殼色漆，後朱漆修補，通體小蛇腹斷。鹿角灰胎，較薄。

琴材配件：木軫，木雁足，紫玉徽。

琴背銘文：(一) 龍池上方刻篆書 "萬壑松風" 四字。

(二) 龍池兩旁刻隸書銘文："昔者參觀古物陳列所，得見晉王微之琴，形式音韻均稱絕品，艷羨不置，而此琴與之極相類。余得此琴在民國丁卯季秋，余偶得此琴，與王琴相似，初認以其款疑，疑為唐琴。然音韻松潤靈活，不亞於所藏名琴。且軫池下有 "雲谷老人" 印，龍池下有 "水晶子" 印。復加審慎拂視，見龍池右下方有二寸餘焦葉楷書 "大通元年鐘山沈約監製"。字跡隱微，與木色不分，殊難辨認也。案沈約字休文、工詩文，為有梁一代宗師，著述宏福，武帝時官至侍中。則此琴訖今已千三百餘歲矣。其古可知，頗堪珍貴。余深辛有此奇緣。因重加整飾，並附識數語，以俟博雅者鑒之。丁卯季秋古吳吉廠管平志於湘筠館"。

(三) 池下刻有 "水晶子藏" 方印。

(四) 池下刻有 "吉廠"、"管平" 方印。

(五) 軫下刻有 "雲谷老人" 圓印。

(六) 龍池內刻 "大通元年鐘山沈約監製"。

製作特點：仲尼式，桐木製。納音處隆起，琴首鑲大理石為飾。

Guqin "Wanhe Songfeng" (*Qin* with name of Wind in the Pines in Ten Thousand Gullies)

Made in the Ming dynasty (1368–1644)

L: 123.5 cm, T: 4.7 cm

Zhongni (Confucian) style of design

Chestnut color lacquer, repaired later with red lacquer. Fine "snake belly" crack patterns throughout

Various inscriptions, including its name and signature of various people who owned it through the ages

Most recently repaired by twentieth century *qin* master Guan Pinghu

96

古琴 (冰磬)

長 121 厘米，寬 (額 19 厘米，肩 20.5 厘米，尾 15.5 厘米)， 厚 3.9 厘米。

民族：漢族

製作年代：明代 (1368–1644)

漆色斷紋：琴面髹栗殼色漆，鹿角灰胎，蛇腹斷。

琴材配件：木軫、木雁足，雁足呈梅花狀。

琴背銘文：(一) 龍池上書 "冰磬中和" 四字。

　　　　　(二) 龍池兩旁刻行書銘文："宮應商鳴，□玉□金，怡情養性""淳煕丁未秋
　　　　　　　　 社日，晦翁題"。

　　　　　(三) 池下刻 "且平" 二字。

製作特點：仲尼式，桐木製，納音處隆起，繫有紫色長穗。

Guqin "Bing Qing" (Qin with name of "Ice Chime")

Made in the Ming dynasty (1368–1644)

L: 121 cm, T: 3.9 cm

Zhongni (Confucian) style of design

Chestnut color lacquer, with "snake belly" crack patterns

Various inscriptions, including its name and signature of different collectors who
owned it through the ages

氣鳴樂器 AEROPHONES

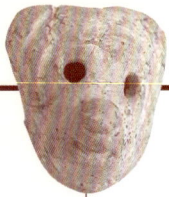

97

十二律隔八相生管

類型：吹奏類正律器

民族：漢族

收藏年代：1960年鄭玉蓀贈。

樂器說明：管狀邊棱類。按氣柱發音原理所用定律法"管律"之正律器。此律管為
銅管，殘，缺黃鐘正副律。所剩各律依次為：大呂＃C、大呂副、太簇
副、太簇D、夾鐘＃D、夾鐘副、姑洗E、姑洗副、仲呂F、仲呂副、
蕤賓＃F、蕤賓副、林鐘副、林鐘G、夷則＃G、夷則副、南呂A、南
呂副、無射副、無射＃A、應鐘B、應鐘副。

功能：正律器

Pitch pipes

Found among the Han people

A set of 22 pipes tuned to the chromatic scale, equivalent to the Western
(relative) pitches of C# to B. Missing the fundamental pitch pipe of the
Haungzhong (C). Each pitch has a duplicate pipe.

Missing two pipes of *Huangzhong* pitch

Used for tuning instruments

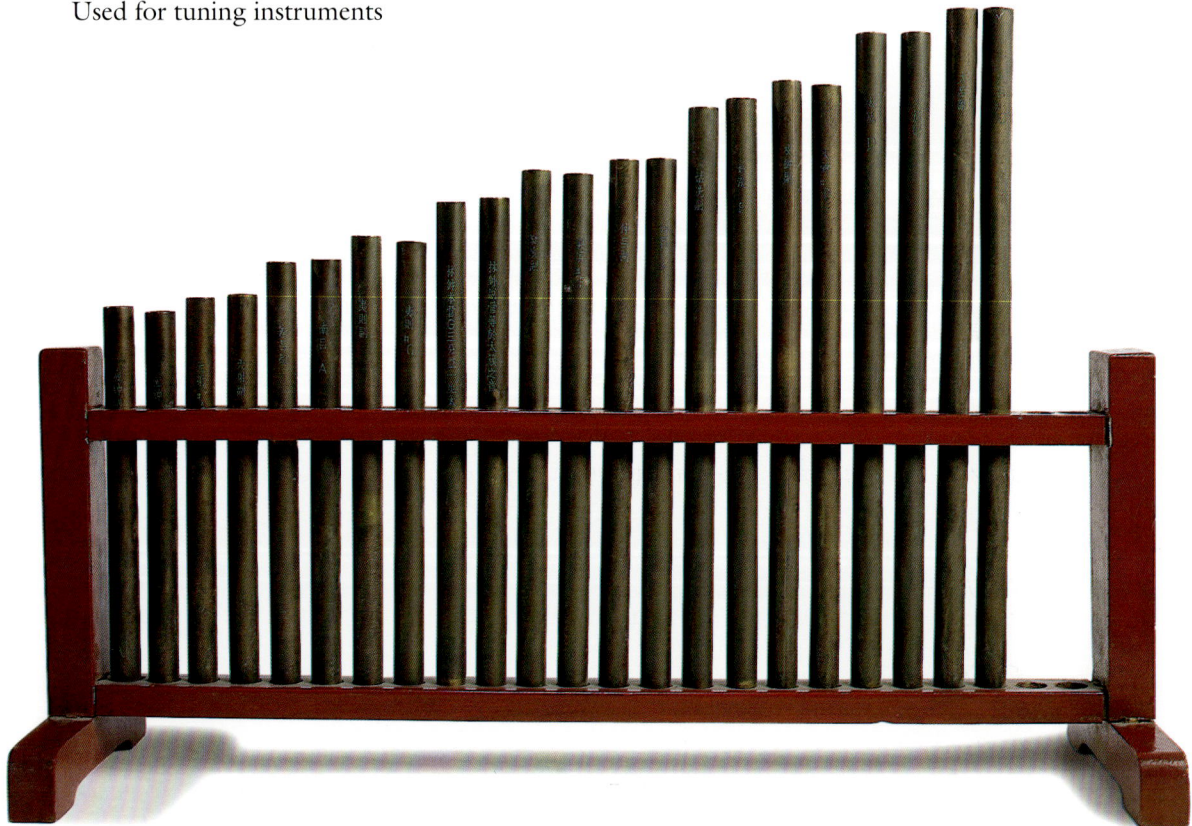

98

彩塤

類型：吹奏樂器

民族：漢族

製作年代：清代 (1644–1911)

收藏年代：傳世品。原為京劇大師梅蘭芳收藏，並於 1953 年捐贈本所。

樂器説明：陶製容器狀邊棱類。形體為平底卵形。六音孔 (前四後二)。通體髹紅漆，
描繪金龍和雲紋。是清代宮廷所使用的樂器。高8.5厘米，腹徑7厘米。

演奏方法：直接吹奏，指法有顫音、打音、抹音等技巧。

功能：先民用以誘捕獵物，現成為旋律樂器。

Caixun (Painted ocarina)

Found among the Han people

Made in the Qing dynasty (1644–1911)

A gift from Mei Lanfang

H: 8.5 cm, D of belly: 7 cm

Used for solo and ensemble music, or to accompany singing

99

三彩釉陶哨

類型：吹奏樂器
民族：漢族
製作年代：宋代 (960–1279)
收藏年代：傳世品。盛家倫遺物，1958 年捐贈本所。
樂器説明：陶製容器狀邊棱類。形體為人頭狀。三孔，高 4 厘米，腹徑 3.7 厘米。
演奏方法：直接吹奏，指法有顫音、打音、抹音等技巧。
功能：先民用以誘捕獵物，現為單純樂器。

Sancai-glazed *Taoxiao* (Three-colour glazed clay whistle)

Found among the Han people
Made in the Song dynasty (960–1279)
A gift from Sheng Jialun
H: 4 cm, D of belly: 3.7 cm
Used for solo and ensemble music, or to accompany singing

100

怪異人頭瓦口哨

類型：吹奏樂器

民族：漢族

製作年代：宋代 (960–1279)

收藏年代：1959 年本所得於振環閣金石瓷陶部。

樂器説明：陶製容器狀邊棱類。三孔，形體為人頭狀。高 4 厘米，腹徑 3.5 厘米。

演奏方法：直接吹奏，指法有顫音、打音、抹音等技巧。

功能：先民用以誘捕獵物，現為單純樂器。

Wakouxiao (Whistle made of baked clay in the shape of an ogre)

Found among the Han people

Made in the Song dynasty (960–1279)

H: 4 cm, D of belly: 3.5 cm

Used for solo and ensemble music, or to accompany singing

101

鬼頭塤

類型：吹奏樂器
民族：漢族
製作年代：宋代 (960–1279)
收藏年代：傳世品。王善賞 1959 年捐贈。
樂器說明：塤體呈鬼頭狀。三孔，高 5.7 厘米，腹徑 4.6 厘米。
演奏方法：直接吹奏，指法有顫音、打音、抹音等技巧。
功能：先民用以誘捕獵物，現為單純樂器。

Guitou Xun (Ocarina in the shape of a devil's head)
Found among the Han people
Made in the Song dynasty (960–1279)
A gift from Wang Shanshang
H: 5.7 cm, D of belly: 4.6 cm
Used for solo and ensemble music, or to accompany singing

102

鳳簫　又名洞簫、雅簫、頌簫、籟、比竹、參差、鳳簫、雲簫

類型：吹奏樂器

民族：漢族等

製作年代：清代 (1644–1911)

收藏年代：傳世品。傅惜華 1959 年捐贈。

樂器說明：竹木製雙翼筏狀邊棱類。十六管，管分左右兩列。管外有木架外殼，髹 黑漆，描繪金龍，正中繪有"鳳簫"二字。高 34 厘米，寬 38 厘米。

演奏方法：多管豎吹

功能：古代用於宮廷雅樂。

Fengxiao **(Phoenix flute)**

End-blown panpipe of 16 bamboo pipes, also known as dongxiao, yaxiao, and other names

Made in the Qing dynasty (1644–1911)

Found among the Han and other people

H: 34 cm, W: 38 cm

Used for court ritual music

103

排簫 又名洞簫、雅簫、頌簫、籟、比竹、參差、鳳簫、雲簫

類型：吹奏樂器

民族：漢族

收藏年代：1965 年

樂器説明：竹製單翼筏狀邊棱類。二十管，高 19.3 厘米，寬 24.5 厘米。

演奏方法：多管豎吹

功能：古代用於宮廷雅樂。

Paixiao (**Panpipe**)

Found among the Han people

Panpipe of 20 bamboo pipes

H: 19.3 cm, W: 24.5 cm

Used for court ritual music

104

龍頭笛

類型：吹奏樂器

民族：漢族、蒙古族、滿族

製作年代：清代 (1644–1911)

收藏年代：1958 年

樂器說明：竹製管狀邊棱類。通體髹紅漆，描繪金龍。尾殘。全長 70 厘米，
　　　　　管身有 1 個吹孔，9 個按音孔。

演奏方法：橫吹

功能：用於宮廷雅樂。

Longtou Di **(Flute with dragon's head)**

Found among the Han people, Mongolians and Manchus

Made in the Qing dynasty (1644–1911)

Side-blown bamboo pipe

L: 70 cm

Used for court ritual music

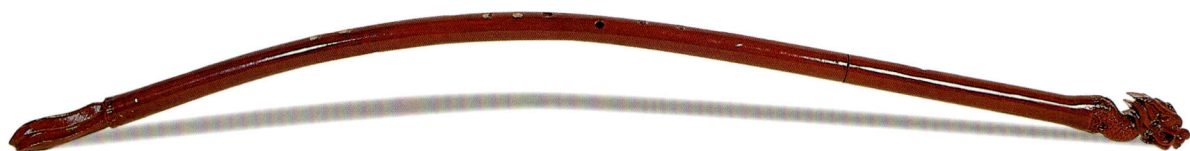

105

龍頭弓笛

類型：吹奏樂器

民族：漢族等

收藏年代：1988 年。為四川成都民族樂團胡結續與雲南民族樂器製作師楊聲，根據大足石刻 (唐代) 中演奏圖研製而成。

樂器說明：竹製管狀邊棱類。形似彎弓，有雌雄之分。雌笛雕鳳頭龍尾，雄笛雕龍頭鳳尾，取吉祥之意。此笛為雄笛，木製，通體呈紫紅色。管身有一個吹孔，九個按孔。全長 113.5 厘米。

演奏方法：橫吹

功能：用於宮廷雅樂。

Longtou Gongdi **(Flute in the shape of a bow with dragon's head)**

Found among the Han people

Replica of a Tang-dynasty stone carving of Dazu, Sichuan province

Side-blown wooden pipe

L: 113.5 cm

Used for court ritual music

106

洞巴

類型：吹奏樂器

民族：景頗族

收藏年代：20世紀60年代初

樂器說明：木製管狀簧振類。上細下粗，由三節組成，下端
　　　　　無喇叭口。節間設銅製插座，上繪有花鳥圖案。
　　　　　管身前開四孔，後開一孔，全長62.4厘米。

演奏方法：豎吹。左手拇指按背孔，食指、中指、無名指按
　　　　　上三孔，右手食指、中指按下兩孔，口含簧哨，
　　　　　吹氣鼓簧發音。

功能：用於喪葬禮儀或在守雀、放牧、過年、吃新米時演
　　　奏。並為傳統歌舞"目腦縱歌"樂隊中的主奏樂器。

Dongba (Reed pipe)

Found among the Jingpo people

Endblown double-reed instrument made of wood, five
finger holes

L: 62.4 cm

Used in funeral rites and many calendrical and other
festivals

107

大管 又稱低音管

類型：吹奏樂器

民族：漢族

收藏年代：1958 年

樂器說明：木製管狀簧振類。管身開八個音孔 (前七後一)。
管長 35.2 厘米，管徑 2.7 厘米。

演奏方法：豎吹。雙手按孔，口含管哨，吹氣發聲。各種管
可更換不同的哨子升降音高。

功能：用於河北吹歌、冀東吵子會、山西八大套、西安鼓樂
等北方笙管樂合奏及戲曲、宗教音樂中。亦用於現代
民族樂隊。

Daguan (Large pipe)

Found among the Han people

Endblown double-reed instrument, eight finger holes,
low-range model of the *xiaoguan* (see No. 108)

L: 35.2 cm, D: 2.7 cm

Used in many kinds of instrumental ensembles in the
Hebei, Shanxi, and Shandong provinces, and in operas
and religious rituals; also used in modern Chinese
orchestras

108

小管　又稱高音管

類型：吹奏樂器

民族：漢族

收藏年代：20世紀50年代初

樂器說明：木製管狀簧振類。管身開九個音孔(前七後二)。
　　　　　據文獻考，九孔管為唐代遺製。管長18厘米，
　　　　　管徑2厘米。

演奏方法：豎吹。雙手按孔，口含管哨，吹氣發聲。各種管
　　　　　可更換不同的哨子升降音高。

功能：用於河北吹歌、冀東吵子會、山西八大套、西安鼓樂
　　　等北方笙管樂合奏及戲曲、宗教音樂中。亦用於現代
　　　民族樂隊。

Xiaoguan (Small pipe)

Found among the Han people

Endblown double-reed instrument, nine finger holes,
possible descendent from the Tang dynasty

L: 18 cm, D: 2 cm

Used in many kinds of instrumental ensembles in the
Hebei, Shanxi, and Shandong provinces, and in operas
and religious rituals; also used in modern Chinese
orchestras

109

海螺 又名蠡、梵貝、海螺號、法螺等

類型：吹奏樂器

民族：藏、蒙古、納西、傣、滿、漢等民族。

製作年代：清乾隆年間 (1736–1795)

樂器說明：容器狀唇振類。此貝為乾隆年間 (1736–1795) 所製，取天然生長的
青白色海螺，磨平螺尖鑲嵌銅吹嘴；螺身鑲嵌銅片為飾，一面鏤刻
精美花紋，一面刻 "乾隆御製" 四字；全長 35 厘米。

演奏方法：左手持螺尾，嘴含吹口，吹氣發音。

功能：古代北方少數民族在軍事、勞動和娛樂生活中演奏。現用於召集群眾及
樂隊中的色彩性樂器。並為藏傳佛教法器。

Hailuo (**Conch shell**)

Made in the Qianlong period (1736–1795) of Qing dynasty

Found among the Tibetans, Mongolians, Naxi, Tai, Manchurians, and
Han people

L: 35 cm

Used in the past by northern nomadic people in military exercises, physical
labor, and relaxation; also used in Tibetan Buddhist rituals

110

海螺 又名蠡、梵貝、海螺號、法螺等

類型：吹奏樂器

民族：藏、蒙古、納西、傣、滿、漢等民族。

收藏年代：傳世品，原為京劇大師梅蘭芳收藏，1953年捐贈本所。

樂器說明：此貝用青白色帶黃斑花條紋的天然海螺製作。全長30厘米，吹口徑2.5厘米，出音口徑16 x 11厘米。

演奏方法：左手持螺尾，嘴含吹口，吹氣發音。

功能：古代北方少數民族在軍事、勞動和娛樂生活中演奏。現用於召集群眾及樂隊中的色彩性樂器。並為藏傳佛教法器。

Hailuo (Conch shell)

Found among the Tibetans, Mongolians, Naxi, Tai, Manchurians, and Han people

A gift from Mei Lanfang

L: 30 cm

Used in the past by northern nomadic people in military exercises, physical labor, and relaxation; also used in Tibetan Buddhist rituals

111

方笙

類型：吹奏樂器

民族：漢族

收藏年代：20世紀50年代初

樂器説明：管狀簧振類。笙斗呈長方形。結構與圓鬥笙相同。
　　　　　裝笙管十四根，一管一音，排列為兩排三列。笙斗
　　　　　木製，全長72.7厘米。

演奏方法：雙手捧扶笙斗，左右手指可插入前後兩排笙管之間
　　　　　的空隙按音，嘴對吹口吹吸發音。

功能：流行於河北、山東、河南、安徽等地，用於民間器樂
　　　演奏和地方戲曲伴奏。

***Fangsheng* (Square mouth organ)**

Found among the Han people

Fourteen bamboo pipes over wooden rectangular
resonance chamber

L: 72.7 cm

Used in folk instrumental ensemble and in opera

112

十七簧笙

類型：吹奏樂器

民族：漢族

收藏年代：20世紀50年代初

樂器説明：竹木製管狀簧振類，笙斗呈圓形。笙管十七根，
　　　　　全長80厘米。

演奏方法：雙手捧扶笙斗，左右手指分別按笙管按孔，嘴對
　　　　　吹口吹吸發音。常用技法有抹音、滑音、頓音、
　　　　　花舌、呼舌、揉音、和喉音等。

功能：用於民間器樂演奏和地方戲曲伴奏。

Shiqihuangsheng (17-pipe mouth organ)

Found among the Han people

Seventeen bamboo pipes over wooden half-spherical
resonance chamber

L: 80 cm

Used in folk instrumental ensemble and in opera

113

銅簫

類型：吹奏樂器

民族：漢族

收藏年代：1965 年

樂器說明：銅製管狀邊棱類。簫管前開五孔，後開一孔。全長 59.7 厘米，管徑 1.9 厘米。

演奏方法：豎吹

功能：獨奏、合奏。

Tongxiao (Copper endblown flute)

Found among the Han people

Copper endblown flute with six finger holes

L: 59.7 cm, D: 1.9 cm

Used in solo and ensemble music

114

銅笛

類型：吹奏樂器

民族：漢族

製作年代：傳世品。擬為唐代 (618–907)。

收藏年代：原為南海琴家、收藏家招學庵舊藏。曾見載於《今虞琴刊》(1937 年)，後於
1947 年送交琴學大師查阜西，並有"寶劍贈烈士"附言 (見《查阜西琴學文
萃》)。後為本所收藏。

樂器說明：銅製管狀邊棱類。管身開十孔，刻有銘文"開元四年"字樣。管長 61.8 厘米，
外徑 1.8 厘米。

演奏方法：橫吹

功能：獨奏、合奏。

Tongdi (Copper sideblown flute)

Found among the Han people

Possibly made in the Tang dynasty (618–907)

Copper sideblown flute with ten finger holes; engravings of "Fourth year of the Kaiyuan reign" of the Tang dynasty (716)

L: 61.8 cm

Used in solo and ensemble music

115

鐵笛

類型：吹奏樂器

民族：漢族

收藏年代：傳世品

樂器說明：鐵製管狀邊棱類。管身開十孔。管長62厘米，外徑2厘米。

演奏方法：橫吹

功能：獨奏、合奏。

Tiedi **(Iron sideblown flute)**

Found among the Han people

Iron endblown flute with ten finger holes

L: 62 cm

Used in solo and ensemble music

116
姐妹簫 又稱占得息、咪咪

類型：吹奏樂器

民族：苗族、布依族。

收藏年代：1958 年

樂器說明：竹製雙管邊棱類。由兩只長短、粗細、音高相同的六孔竹製簫管組成。上
端管口置入木塞，內側削一溝槽，與管壁形成吹口。管身開六個按孔。管
身背面距離管端 3 厘米處開一音孔。全長 41 厘米，外徑 1.2 厘米。

演奏方法：可捆紮兩管，也可分為單管吹奏。奏時口含管頭豎吹，左手無名指、中
指、食指按兩管下三孔，右手無名指、中指、食指按兩管上三孔，可吹奏
雙音和簡單的支聲音調。

功能：可獨奏並用於青年愛情生活。

Jiemei Xiao ("Sister" endblown flute)
Found among the Miao and Buyi people

Bamboo endblown double flute with two identical pipes, six finger holes on
each

L: 41 cm

Used as solo performance and for courtship among young people

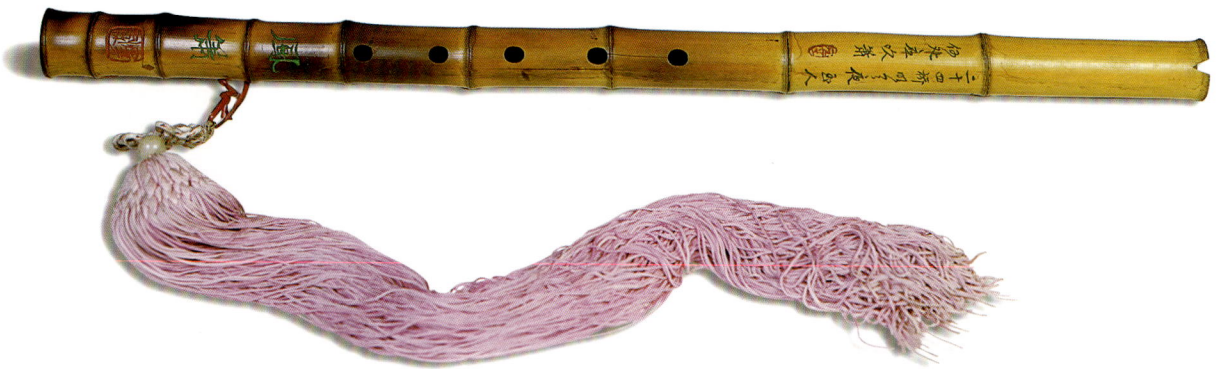

117

尺八　又稱洞簫

類型：吹奏樂器

民族：漢族

收藏年代：1963 年

樂器說明：竹製管狀邊棱類。流行於福建省和台灣地區。竹製。正面開五個按音孔，
　　　　　背面開一個按音孔。帶絲穗。音色和演奏方法與簫相似，但音量較大。管
　　　　　長 62 厘米，口徑 3.8 厘米。

演奏方法：豎吹。有敲音、顫音、上倚音、下倚音等技巧。

功能：是福建南音的主奏樂器之一。在閩南語系的鄉劇、梨園戲、高甲戲、台灣歌仔
　　　戲中均有使用。

Chiba or *Dongxiao* (Endblown flute)

Found among the Han people

Bamboo pipe with six finger holes

L: 62 cm, D: 3.8 cm

Major instrument for the *Nanyin* ensemble of Fujian; used in various regional operas in Fujian and Taiwan provinces

118

曲笛　又稱橫笛、班笛、紫線笛、蘇笛

類型：吹奏樂器

民族：漢族

收藏年代：1964 年

樂器説明：竹製管狀邊棱類。管身開吹孔、膜孔各一個，按音孔六個，前出音孔一個
和後出音孔二個。管長 61.5 厘米，外徑 2.2 厘米。

演奏方法：橫吹

功能：用於江南絲竹、蘇南吹打、潮州笛套鑼鼓和昆曲伴奏等。

Qudi ("Opera" sideblown flute)

Found among the Han people

Bamboo pipe with six finger holes, one blow hole, one membrane hole, and
three structural holes

L: 61.5 cm

Used in Kun opera, Jiangnan Sizhu ensemble music, Sunan wind music, and
Chaozhou ensemble music

119

玉屏簫

類型：吹奏樂器

民族：漢族

收藏年代：1958年

樂器説明：竹製管狀邊棱類。因採集貴州省玉屏等地所產小水竹製作而名。管身開六個橢圓形音孔 (前五後一)，下端背面有出音孔，孔壁向內呈25度斜面，使音色圓潤柔和動聽。管身外表塗古銅色，雕有花紋及詩詞。全長 64.5 厘米，管身呈橢圓形 (是人工夾扁) 管徑 1.7 、 1.5 厘米。

演奏方法：豎吹

功能：常用於江南絲竹、廣東音樂等民間器樂合奏，戲曲伴奏中。

Yupingxiao (Yuping endblown flute)

Found among the Han people

Bamboo endblown flute made by a special bamboo species in Yuping of Guizhou province, six oval-shaped finger holes

L: 64.5 cm

Used in Jiangnan Sizhu ensemble music, Guangdong ensemble music, and opera

120

鷹骨笛　又稱鷹笛、骨笛

類型：吹奏樂器

民族：藏族

收藏年代：傳世品。1998 年採集於青海湟中。

樂器說明：骨製管狀邊棱類。用大鷹的翅骨製成。管內中空，兩端皆通，管身
　　　　　有七孔。全長 25.9 厘米，管徑 1.8 厘米。

演奏方法：豎吹。雙手執管下端，口半含管口，以舌尖堵住管口的一部分形成
　　　　　氣口，按孔吹奏。

功能：自娛

Yinggu Di (**Eagle-bone flute**)

Found among the Tibetan people

Collected in Qinghai province

Endblown flute made of wing cartridge of large eagle, seven finger holes

L: 25.9 cm, D: 1.8 cm

Used for leisure playing

121

鷹骨笛

類型：吹奏樂器

民族：藏族

收藏年代：傳世品。 1998 年採集於青海湟中。

樂器說明：骨製管狀邊棱類。管身九孔，管內中空，兩端皆通。全長32厘米，
管徑 2.4 厘米。

演奏方法：豎吹。雙手執管下端，口半含管口，以舌尖堵住管口的一部分形成
氣口，按孔吹奏。

功能：自娛

Yinggu Di (Eagle-bone flute)

Found among the Tibetan people

Collected in Qinghai province

Endblown flute made with wing cartridge of large eagle, nine finger holes

L: 32 cm, D: 2.4 cm

Used for leisure playing

122

木嗩吶　又稱蘇爾奈 (維吾爾)

類型：吹奏樂器

民族：維吾爾族、烏孜別克族。

收藏年代：20世紀60年代

樂器說明：木製管狀簧振類。通體用硬質整木鏇製而成。管身以
　　　　　多種花紋或線紋為飾。管身開八孔 (前七後一)。管上
　　　　　端插葦製雙簧哨片，不設氣牌。全長40厘米。

演奏方法：豎吹

功能：用於獨奏、鼓吹樂合奏或歌舞伴奏。

Mu Suona (Wooden shawm)

Found among the Uighur and Uzbek people

Wooden double-reeded pipe with eight finger holes and no flaring horn

L: 40 cm

Used for solo and ensemble music and to accompany singing and dancing

古樂風流

123

小嗩吶　又稱喇叭、海笛

類型：吹奏樂器

民族：漢族

收藏年代：1963 年

樂器說明：木製管狀簧振類。由杆、哨、氣牌、侵子、和碗構成。杆用紅木製成，為空心圓錐體，上開八個 (前七後一) 圓形音孔。杆身全長 40 厘米，碗高 7 厘米，碗徑 8 厘米。

演奏方法：豎吹

功能：廣泛應用於器樂演奏、戲曲伴奏和婚喪喜慶活動。

Xiao Suona (Small shawm)

Found among the Han people

Wooden double-reeded pipe with eight finger holes and flaring horn

L: 40 cm

Used in ensemble performance, operas, and in wedding and funeral rituals